This book
is dedicated
to my colleagues at
The Honolulu Advertiser;
the most talented, hard working, fiercely individualistic and closely knit
family of writers, editors, photographers, artists and support staff in the pacific:

Dick Adair, Wanda Adams, Ilene Aleshire, Richard Ambo, Dennis Anderson, Amelia Ang, Helen Aoki, Jane Arita, Bart Asato, Bruce Asato, Robert Bakutis, John Bender, Jim Borg, Ferd Borsch, Tom Buchanan, Jerry Burris, Lynne Chang, George Chaplin, Don Chapman, Robert Cheng, Hugh Clark, Robert Collias, Beverly Creamer, Linda Dalrymple, Kevin Dayton, Paul deVille, Jim Dooley, Joe Edwards, Marcie Farias, Pat Fong, Bill Froloff, Halili Garcia, Philip Gialanella, Paula Gillingham, Pat Glaser, Stu Glauberman, Melvin Goo, John Griffin, Wayne Harada, Anne Harpham, Marshall Hughes, Cindy Hirayama, Will Hoover, Esme Infante, Monte Ito, Ron Jett, Jamie Kamezawa, Tom Kaser, Leslie Kawamoto, Gerry Keir, Gwen Kekaula–Ching, Ed Kennedy, Steve Kimura, Ken Kobayashi, Dave Koga, Bill Kresnak, Vic Laniauskas, Mike Leidemann, Ferd Lewis, Kay Lynch, Mark Matsunaga, Patsy Matsuura, Terry McMurray, Mike Middlesworth, Ann Miller, Becky Minter, Mary Mitsuda, Clyde Mizumoto, Curtis Murayama, Ernie Murphy, Gail Nakamura, Helen North, Charles Okamura, Vickie Ong, Sandra Oshiro, Rick Padden, Loraine Pang, David Polhemus, Stan Pusieski, Dave Reardon, Jim Richardson, Catherine Richey, Ronn Ronck, Peter Rosegg, Brian Saunders, Kitty Saunders, Wade Shirkey, Kit Smith, Sharon Smith, John Strobel, Dan Stebbins, Jimmy Takamiya, Ed Tanji, Greg Taylor, Jan Tenbruggencate, Steven Tsai, David Twigg–Smith, Desmond Twigg–Smith, Thurston Twigg–Smith, Peter Ucko, Ken Uemura, Takashi Umeda, Curtis Uno, Vicki Viotti, Carl Viti, David Waite, Greg Wiles, Walt Wright, David Yamada, Andy Yamaguchi, Greg Yamamoto, Stanley Yamashita, Susan Yim, Milton Yokota, Debra Yuen and Ellsworth Zahm.

OUR HAWAII

THE BEST OF BOB KRAUSS

Produced and published by
ISLAND HERITAGE PUBLISHING

Cover photograph, **Richard Peterson**
Illustrations, **Calley O'Neill**
Cover design, **Paul Turley**
Book design, **Paul Turley** & **Dixon Smith**
Project Director, **Dixon Smith**

First Edition
First Printing, 1990
Copyright ©1990 Island Heritage Publishing
Please address orders and correspondence to:
ISLAND HERITAGE PUBLISHING
A division of The Madden Corporation
99-880 Iwaena Street
Aiea, Hawaii 96701
(808) 487-7299

ISBN 0-89610-166-5

Printed in Hong Kong

O U R
HAWAII

THE BEST OF BOB KRAUSS

Contents

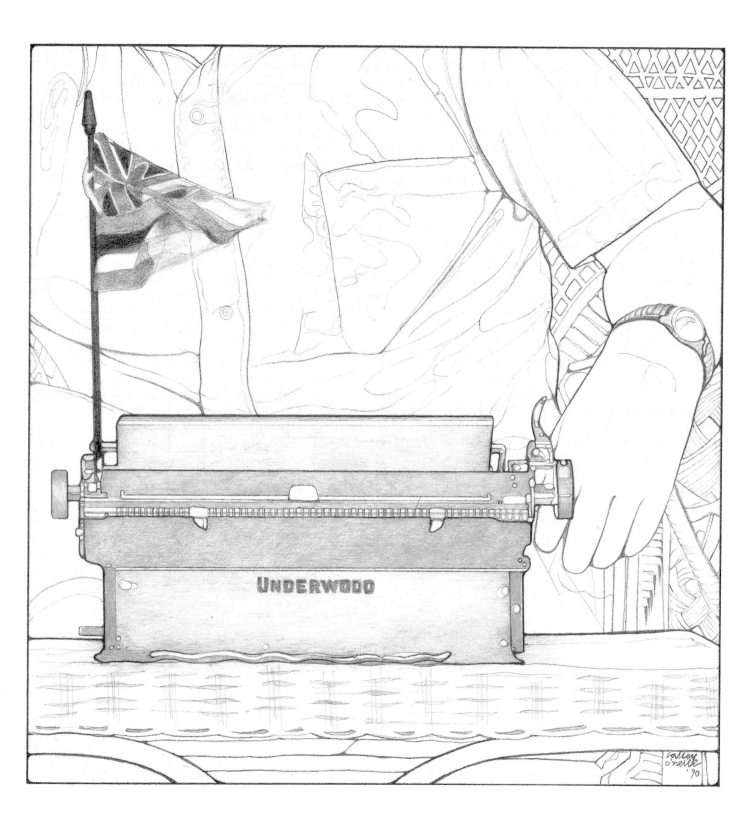

The Truth About Aloha

In the days of old Hawaii, Children of the Land established a noble tradition designed to perpetuate their identities. The tradition holds that each Child of the Land or *kamaaina* should absorb the folklore, the values, the history and customs and oddities of his or her place. Then, at the proper time, the kamaaina should pass on this knowledge to a chosen person so that the soul of Hawaii will not be lost. You will have to decide for yourself whether or not you wish to be chosen.

Naturally, each Child of the Land has different memories. No two kamaainas take exactly the same approach about what is the REAL Hawaii. That's what makes it so much fun. There is constant disagreement about the finer points. It's like comparing recipes or the strengths and weaknesses of your favorite football teams.

My frame of reference is that of a scribbler of stories for *The Honolulu Advertiser* and for books about Hawaii. Actually, a Child of the Land should be born in the Islands. My parents, unfortunately, neglected to provide me with this qualification. I've tried to make up for it by forty years of chasing around Hawaii and the Pacific asking people questions about themselves and writing down the answers.

The first thing I learned was the real meaning of Aloha. Friendly natives invited me to a party soon after I arrived in Honolulu which was a long time ago during the administration of President Harry Truman in a bygone age when airplanes still had propellers. At the party, I met a fellow who had voted for Dewey. I pointed out the error of his ways and we got into an argument. It was with considerable self-gratification that I told him where he could go and what he could do with his politics.

About a month later I was invited to another party. Who should show up but the same person I had insulted previously. It was very embarrassing. To make it worse, I discovered he was much more important than I had supposed. It was my first lesson in how to survive on an island where we are all vulnerable to one another and where it is usually smarter to be polite than right. That's the aloha spirit.

In 1973 during the administration of Richard Nixon I learned a lot more lessons about aloha. In that year a group of middle-aged adventurers including me set out to retrace the historic route of missionary William Ellis around the Big Island of Hawaii on the 150th anniversary of his expedition. We hiked, sailed and paddled 300 miles in thirty days.

My most vivid aloha lesson came while we were paddling our outrigger canoe down the placid Kona Coast past a stretch of impassable lava wilderness. I had never paddled a canoe before. Our steersman, Tommy Holmes, now executive director of the Hawaiian Maritime Center, explained that the important thing is to stroke in synchronization. He was right. The canoe moved sluggishly when we did not coordinate our strokes. But when each paddle moved as one, the canoe leaped forward with a dramatic surge of power.

I could feel it in the seat of my pants. It was very exciting. Each perfectly synchronized stroke unleashed a mysterious power stronger than the muscles in all of our arms. That sense of power was heady and addicting; to be part of it made me pull harder. I lost myself in the excitement until Tommy's voice came sharply from the stern, "Keep the stroke, Bob." In this magic of motion, I had strayed off into my own rhythm. Sometimes, when we held the stroke for a long time, the experience was too intense to be contained. "Eeeeeeeeyah!" shouted one of the paddlers at the bow. I felt the same way so I let out a mild, "Yipee." That's the aloha spirit.

By this time I'm on my third generation of readers, still trying to keep pace with the unique, evolving identity of our Hawaii. This book is a collection of the best stories I've written for *The Honolulu Advertiser* in the last few years so it is about Hawaii today, not the way it was forty years ago. It contains more of the future folklore of the Islands than that of the past. But there are anchors of continuity that don't change, like the Aloha Spirit. And how you become a Child of the Land. It happens when you begin to care about the Islands and the people you live with.

This is not a guide book about where to go and what to see. It's a true story book about how we live. I hope these more than seventy true stories will provide for local residents a handy reference to our modern folklore. The biggest compliment you can pay me is to steal these stories, tell them to others as if they were your own and keep them alive. For visitors, I hope this book provides an opportunity to get out of the tour bus and into the homes of real people who live here. This book is written to help give meaning to the things you see and the people you meet in Hawaii.

You can approach this book as you would a family album of word pictures. So it doesn't matter whether you start in the middle, at the end or begin at the beginning. It's like an island, all part of one whole. I hope you enjoy the time you spend between the covers of *Our Hawaii*.

Little Known Great Moments in Hawaiian History

How The *Shaka* Sign Got Started

Among the expressive gestures that have come down to us in the course of civilization are the thumbs up and thumbs down signs given by the mob at the Colosseum in Rome during the days of Caesar, the "V for victory" sign flashed by prime minister Winston Churchill from bomb-ravaged London during World War II, and the *shaka* sign in Hawaii. Politicians seeking reelection in Honolulu waggle the shaka sign from roadsides at passing motorists to show that they are just plain folks. Bronzed surfers give the shaka sign at one another in manly gestures of friendly fraternity. Children all over Honolulu eagerly throw grins and the shaka sign at TV cameras hoping to appear as signatures on television newscast sign-offs.

Ever since anybody here can remember, the shaka sign has been a local logo, a universal gesture of good will, a confirmation that everything is all right and that we are friends, you and me. Residents of Honolulu had been casting the shaka sign, a fist with pinky and thumb extended, for years before they began to wonder how it started in the first place. This led to intensive research at cocktail parties and on the 19th hole of golf courses, and to considerable disagreement among the researchers who all consider themselves experts on the folklore of Honolulu.

One school contends that the shaka sign originated among marble shooters during grade school recess sometime in the 1930s. The approved method of shooting was with the little finger extended as the thumb snapped forward, hence the shaka sign. Another theory credits used car salesman Lippy Espinda, who made popular television commercials back in the 1960s, with flashing the first shaka sign.

The discovery of a photograph dated 1906 threw all shaka sign scholars into a tizzy because it showed newsboys of the Hawaiian newspaper, *Ke Aloha Aina*, posed in front of the printing plant and one of the boys appeared to be making the shaka sign. It turned out later that he was merely picking his nose with his little finger. The excitement subsided.

In 1985 a woman of Japanese descent called me at *The Advertiser* with another theory: "We were reading your story about the shaka sign and my son said, 'Mama, that's Shakanuma, the Buddha who prayed with his fingers folded except for the pinky and thumb.' I remember my grandparents saying 'shaka,' to mean 'praise the Lord,' like when someone does something nice. It means a happy thought. My grandparents made the gesture with the hand on the heart, not raised up. It goes back to the 1880s."

Robert Aitken, a teacher at Diamond Sangha, a Zen Buddhist Society, agreed that "Shayka" is pronounced, "shaka" and that Shakyamuni is the name of the historical Buddha. But he added, "I've never heard of this as the origin of the slang expression. I remember the shaka sign very well from my youth when I worked at the pineapple cannery. There was so much noise on the line we had to talk with hand signals. The shaka sign meant 'I agree' or 'I understand.' It was done with the hand raised high. There were signs for going to the bathroom and for going to lunch. This was made with motions like eating soup."

It is with becoming humility that I can now tell you confidently how the shaka sign REALLY started. The great moment of discovery came in the village of Laie on the other side of the island in December of 1985. I had gone there to consult Marilyn Fonoimoana, a school teacher, and her friend, Hanaloa Nihipali, who had promised to reveal the secret. Marilyn said the shaka sign began as a blessing to the congregation of the Mormon Church by one of the elders,

Hamana Kalili, a fisherman of renown. When it was his turn to lead the service, he would lift his powerful arms and urge the congregation to rise.

Before Marilyn could finish, Hanaloa broke in.

"As a little girl, I remember his right hand," she said. "Three fingers were cut off. Just the thumb and little finger were left. Everybody knew what he would do when we all stood up. He would smile and say, 'Right on!' with his hand up in the air. People used to chuckle because he didn't speak very well."

Lucy Marasco, the granddaughter of Pele Kaio who worked with Kalili on Kahuku Plantation, said the kids in Laie always made the shaka sign when they saw Kalili. "But we didn't say 'shaka' in those days," she explained. "We said, 'Hamana D.A.' It means, 'Right on the kini popo.'"

Walter Wong, whose grandfather's mother was a sister of Kalili's mother, said his great-uncle was a champion fisherman whose son swam with Duke Kahanamoku, the surfing pioneer, and other beach boys at Waikiki. "The beach boys would come to Hamana's *hukilau* (fishing party) in Laie," Wong said. "That's how the shaka sign spread around. It means, 'Right on the kini popo.' Everybody in Laie knew what it meant."

Marilyn said children in Laie also used the 'Hamana D.A.' sign as a warning because Kalili guarded the train of flatcars carrying sugar cane stalks to the mill. Hanaloa couldn't keep still so she broke in again, "The train went right by my house. We kids ran alongside and pulled off the best stalks to take home and eat when Hamana wasn't looking."

Kehau Kawahigashi said she saw Kalili make the shaka sign way back in 1915 when calling the villagers of Laie with upraised arm to his *hukilau*. "In those days everybody brought a sack to carry home fish after they pulled the net on shore," Kawahigashi recalled. "I was five. My grandfather took me along to the *hukilaus*. The more people in the family, the

more fish you bring home." She said Kalili's generosity became legendary and was associated with the image of his upraised arm, middle fingers missing, thumb and little finger prominently extended, as he called people to share his catch.

Like most folk heroes, Kalili is bigger than life to his admirers. One of these is Henry Walker, Jr. for years a top executive in Honolulu as head of Amfac, Inc., a Big Five firm. Henry proudly remembers, as a boy, that Hamana taught him how to throw a fishing net. All of Laie knows that Kalili was the tug or war champion of the Windward Coast. On Laie Day he would invite seven big Samoans to take hold of one end of the rope, tie the other end around his waist and pull the Samoans across the line by himself. Then he dressed up in a cape and a helmet and ruled as King Kamehameha for the rest of the day.

At least three stories are told in Laie by Kalili fans about how he lost his middle fingers. Wong insists that retired fireman Hiwa Lua, who fished with Kalili, said he lost the fingers using dynamite to kill fish. Another story is that a shark bit the fingers off. Marilyn said she got it straight from Easter Logan, Kalili's nephew, that his uncle's fingers were smashed in the rollers at Kahuku Sugar Mill.

The only thing that everybody agrees on is that the 'Hamana D.A.' or 'shaka' sign was known to and used by everybody who lived in Laie and that it meant 'right on,' just as it does today, because they all liked Kalili.

Marilyn said she believes Lippy Espinda, the pidgin-talking used car salesman, picked up the gesture and spread it around the islands on TV. Lippy substituted his own phrase, 'shaka,' for 'Hamana D.A.' Later on, Honolulu Mayor Frank Fasi used the shaka sign as his campaign symbol. Marilyn said she was away when that happened but she immediately thought of Hamana Kalili when she came home and saw the shaka sign during Fasi's next political campaign.

Scientific Revolution in Waikiki

Students of science are familiar with the great discoveries which have thrust Western civilization into the forefront of human achievement. We all know that the theory of evolution, with Charles Darwin as midwife, was born on an island in the Pacific. The theory of heredity, inspired by Gregor Johann Mendel, was born in a pea patch in Czechoslovakia. The theory of relativity, brainchild of Albert Einstein, was born in a physics lab in Germany. So it seems only fitting that the most recent revolution in science, artificial reproduction of a human gene component, reaching into the very mystery of ourselves, was born in a kosher delicatessen in Waikiki.

This startling information about a little known great moment in Hawaiian history came to my attention through the courtesy of Edmund H. Volkart, professor emeritus of sociology at the University of Hawaii. He sent me a clipping from an issue of *Science* magazine in the late 1980s. This article told about a joint U.S.-Japan conference to discuss something called bacterial plasmids in 1972 at the East-West Center. The visiting scientists stayed in Waikiki hotels.

On the night before the conference began, a group of the brainy conferees set out along Kalakaua Avenue to unwind. Their names were Stanley Cohen, Herb Boyer, Stanley Falco, and Charles and Ginger Brinton. The long walk stimulated their appetites. When they came across a delicatessen with a sign in the window that read, "Shalom," they all went in for corned beef.

While they were eating, they got to talking about the experiments each was conducting separately. By the time they finished their corned beef, they had planned the combined experiments that would lead to recombinant DNA. It is a technology that physicist Freeman Dyson said will have a greater impact on civilization than the industrial revolution.

This one is called the bio-technological revolution and Cohen and Boyer are the founders.

There can be no doubt that this is, indeed, a little known great moment in Hawaiian history. But which delicatessen did it happen in?

A recent visitor, who had heard the story, decided to make a pilgrimage to this hallowed shrine of science, to touch the walls and trod the floor. Perhaps the corned beef would inspire another great discovery. If nothing else, the delicatessen could be placed on the National Register of Historic Places. But he couldn't find it. The delicatessen has disappeared amidst the forest of high rise hotels. In place of the delicatessen, he found a yuppie shopping mall. "They've obliterated a piece of history," he wrote *Science*. "And they don't even know it. There isn't even a plaque on the sidewalk."

With the honor of Honolulu at stake, I immediately set out to learn more about this historic kosher-style delicatessen. It wasn't easy.

Dr. Morton Mandel, professor of biochemistry and biophysics at the university, said he was on sabbatical in 1972 but he remembers a place called the New York Deli across from the Ilikai Hotel. That would be a long walk from Kalakaua Avenue all right, like hiking to Acapulco for a taco. But then, maybe scientists are good walkers.

Dr. Mandel said Stanley Cohen had become chairman of the Stanford University Department of Medicine and that Herb Boyer went to the University of California at Berkeley. I called Cohen at Stanford. He said he couldn't remember the name of the deli, what he ate or even how the corned beef tasted because he was so interested in the conversation. He said the only reason the story has become part of the folklore of science is because Stanley Falco told it during an oral history interview at the Massachusetts Institute of Technology. All Cohen could remember is that the delicatessen was on the main thoroughfare of Waikiki. That ruled out the New York Deli.

Fortunately, the late Buck Buchwach, at that time editor in chief of *The Advertiser*, also appreciated kosher-style corned beef. "There was a little place right on Kalakaua Avenue called the Deli," he said. "It was run by a Chinese." Sure enough, in the yellow pages of a 1970 phone book, there is a listing for "THE DELI, Kosher Style Pastrami – Corned Beef, Lox & Bagels, 2232 Kalakaua Ave., between Royal Hawaiian and Seaside Ave."

So we have found the home of the cutting edge of modern science. While the delicatessen itself has vanished, the family of Kenny Chong, the Chinese kosher-style cook who prepared the historic corned beef, is still in business over on the other side of the island. "I don't remember that particular night," said his son, Ernie. "But a university professor used to play his flute while his colleagues discussed Nietzsche over lox and bagels."

When Statehood Hung By A Lei

Statehood for Hawaii has so long been accepted in the length and breadth of the Union that only pre baby-boomers remember the anticipation we felt for that long awaited historic moment which took place, at last, in August of 1959. For more than half a century, residents of Hawaii had paid federal taxes without having a vote in the U.S. Congress. Island residents did not even elect their own governor. He was appointed by the President of the United States, as if we citizens of Hawaii were incapable of governing ourselves.

Politicians of both parties in the Islands argued, pleaded and demanded for years that we be granted full citizenship. But there were always excuses in Congress to delay. Democrats did not want to admit representatives from what was then a solid Republican outpost. The high number of Orientals in Hawaii worried racial bigots. During the era of Senator Eugene McCarthy, super patriots saw Communists under the bed of every labor leader in the Islands.

And so the maneuvering in Washington of Hawaii Delegate to Congress Jack Burns, who finally accomplished the impossible, has been carefully documented by historians. But there is one detail that has been neglected, a little known moment in the history of statehood for Hawaii that deserves to be told. It is the story of a flower lei and a kiss and why the most stubborn opponent to statehood in the U.S. Congress changed his mind. Without that change of heart, we still might not be celebrating Admission Day because the Hawaii statehood bill would have stayed bottled up in the Rules Committee of the U.S. House of Representatives.

This is a story about Hawaii Delegate Jack Burns, of a hula dancer in a sarong and bare feet, and of U.S. Representative Howard Smith, a Democrat and an implacable opponent of statehood for Hawaii. The lady who wore the sarong is Lani O'Connor of Virginia, formerly Lani McMillen of Honolulu, sister of Francis McMillen, chairman of Hawaii's state Board of Education under the Waihee administration.

"I moved to Washington with my husband in 1953," said Lani. "Being an Island girl, I went to pay a visit to the delegate, who was then Betty Farrington. Later, when Jack Burns was elected, I called on him." Lani said she was politically nonpartisan. Both she and her husband supported statehood for Hawaii, so she volunteered to help.

"Delegate Burns would call and ask me to appear for him," she said. "Sometimes, when he and Mrs. Burns entertained, I did the hula at their parties. One day, just prior to the passage of statehood, Delegate Burns called and asked if I would do him a favor. He said the statehood bill was bottled up in Judge Smith's House Rules Committee.

"The delegate was trying to get the bill on the floor of the House for a vote. First he had to get the approval of Judge Smith, a long time foe of statehood and chairman of the committee, to move the bill out of committee to the floor. And it was taking forever. Delegate Burns said to me, 'I think we're going to get the rule (permitting an early vote in the House) and I promised Judge Smith if he gave us the rule I would have a beautiful, sarong–clad, Hawaiian girl give him a kiss and a flower lei.' The delegate asked me to do it and I agreed."

Lani said Burns told her to wait by the telephone because she had to be ready at a moment's notice. She said she waited about three days and every day a fresh lei arrived from Hawaii. "Then Delegate Burns called and said Judge Smith had approved the rule," Lani said. "I was to bring my sarong and lei immediately. I rushed over to the delegate's office and changed there. In my sarong and bare feet, I went with the delegate to Judge Smith's office, which was on the same floor.

"We went in and the delegate said, 'Judge, I'm paying off my debt.' Judge Smith was very poker faced. He always looked as if he had just bitten into a green persimmon. But when we walked in, he broke into a big smile. He was just delighted with his lei and a kiss."

Two days later, on March 12, the House of Representatives convened to vote on the statehood bill. Mary Isa, who was secretary to Jack Burns – both as delegate to Congress and later as governor of Hawaii, said what happened then was Jack Burns' favorite part of the story. He was chatting on the floor with other representatives when Smith came along. The dour Virginian was noted for having no sense of humor. He never cracked a joke. As he passed Burns and the other statehood supporters, he grinned and said, "Well, I got my payoff."

Voyage of the Pregnant Sea Captain

"Who are you, the new cook?" a stevedore on the dock asked Lynn Korwatch as she boarded the Matson container ship *Maui* in Oakland before starting the run to Honolulu. Cook indeed! Korwatch did not head for the galley. She climbed three flights to officers' country where she strode right by the quarters for the third, second and chief mates.

That is because Lynn Korwatch, tanned and confident, was making her first voyage from San Francisco to Honolulu as the first female sea captain in the U.S. merchant marine, truly a little known great moment in Hawaiian history. She was also the first pregnant captain in the U.S. merchant marine. You might say VERY pregnant – as in eight months. According to scuttlebutt in the Matson container yard at Sand Island in Honolulu Harbor, this made the chief mate somewhat nervous because he didn't know the drill for assisting his captain in the delivery of her baby.

The voyage went without a squall from either the weather or an infant and, when it was over, Korwatch received the approval of Robert J. Pfeiffer, chairman of the board and chief executive officer of Alexander & Baldwin, Inc., parent company of Matson Navigation Co. "She earned her spurs," said Pfeiffer, who went to sea in his teens. "Everybody recognizes her professionalism."

Probably the hardest thing about her first voyage as captain of a U.S. flag ship was finding a uniform. Nobody makes uniforms for very pregnant merchant marine sea captains. "It's tough," she admitted as she sat in the master's cabin of the *Maui*. "As a first mate, I just wore Matson coveralls. Maternity uniforms are not available in private stores." She finally called for help from the Navy where female officers have been getting pregnant for some time now.

As captain, Korwatch was in charge of a ship two-and-one-half times as long as a football field with a crew of 34 and a registered weight of 38,800 tons. Three other women worked on board. "One is the chief steward, one is assistant cook and the third a dining room waitress," said Korwatch. "So the stevedore in Oakland made an honest mistake. Most women in the merchant marine are in the stewards departments."

Korwatch said being an officer on a merchant ship is a terrific job for a woman – although the opportunities become more limited as the merchant marine shrinks. "I've read stories about unequal pay for women in other professions," she said. "I've never run into that as a member of the Masters, Mates & Pilots Union." Her pay as captain, set by the union in 1988, was $8,800 per month. "But it's a hard career to get into," she said. "There are fewer and fewer jobs with the major shipping lines. There is still opportunity on tug boats, supply ships, research vessels and tankers."

In order to hold down her job, she has to know celestial navigation and be able to operate the radar, LORAN, radio direction finder and satellite navigation systems. As captain, she has to have a good working knowledge of the ship as well as loading and maintenance. "I certainly don't know enough about the engines to overrule the opinion of the chief engineer," she said. "If worst comes to worst, I go home and ask my husband, who's chief engineer for another shipping company."

Korwatch said her voyages as captain will be few and far between during the next few years because she is a relief captain only. After she had her baby, she went back to being chief mate. She said a permanent job as captain of a Matson ship won't come until a permanent captain retires.

The Cop Who Caught a Squealer

Probably the least known great moment in Hawaiian history happened when a Honolulu police sergeant named Mark Greenwell, an enthusiastic throw net fishermen, caught a screaming, snapping, squirming wild pig in his fish net. At the time, he had no premonition what a great moment in the history of law enforcement this would turn out to be.

Greenwell lived near the top of Pacific Heights next door to the Koolau Mountains where wild pigs still roam. In the mid-eighties, a family of pigs moved into town and began rooting up the steeply sloping back yards of Pacific Heights residents. That was when Sergeant Greenwell went into action. He admitted, "They're not going to believe me at the station," as he contemplated the ruin of his tattered net.

He said the pigs showed up at about 7 A.M. A mother and a dozen *keikis* (piglets) were digging in his garden. "I didn't want to shoot them," he explained. "The only thing I could think of was to grab my throw net. I sneaked out to the landing. They were right below me, about ten feet down. I threw the net and got the mother and two or three other little pigs. She went right through the net. There were squealing pigs all over the place. Another one went through the net here. This one got rolled up in it. He only weighs about ten or 20 pounds and he doesn't have any teeth but he's a mean little guy. Try to pat him and he'll snap your hand off."

Greenwell held up the vicious little beast by its hind legs. He said he believes pig hunters drove the family up from Pauoa Flats. Next door neighbor David White added, "This family of wild pigs has been around for about a month. I built a fence to keep them out. People throw rocks at them. They're such a nuisance and they're very destructive."

Speaking as a fisherman, Greenwell said catching a pig in his net was a great moment. So far as he knows, nobody has ever fished up a pig before. "You know, you really get excited the first time," he admitted. "I remember how I felt the first time I caught a shark, and an ulua. Now I've caught my first pig." He said he planned to give the prize to his brother, who has a ranch in Haleiwa, to be raised until the pig is big enough to be the main course at a *luau*.

It was at this point that the State Division of Conservation & Resource Enforcement got into the case. They discovered that Greenwell had been hunting without a license. James Kekuchi, who handled hunting violations in downtown Honolulu, went to the police station where he tracked down the intrepid pig fisherman. "I couldn't believe it," said the police sergeant. "But he was serious. I asked him what I was supposed to do with wild pigs rooting up my back yard. He said I was supposed to get a permit. I asked him how I could do that at 7 o'clock in the morning. It really surprised me."

Maurice Matsuzaki, chief of the enforcement division, pointed out that Greenwell broke two regulations by catching the pig with his fish net up in Pacific Heights. 1. Hunting without a license. 2. Trapping without a permit. Each violation is a petty misdemeanor which carries a maximum penalty of six months in jail and a $500 fine.

Matsuzaki said he spotted the possible violations while reading my story in *The Advertiser*. His division immediately swung into action, checking with the Division of Forestry & Wildlife to see if a hunting license had been issued to Greenwell before he threw the fish net. An annual license costs $7.50. No such license had been issued. Nor had Greenwell bothered to obtain a permit to trap wild animals. "The story may have been humorous to some people but we have to investigate," said Matsuzaki. "When people read the story, they might ask us, 'What are you going to do about it?' Just because he's a police officer doesn't mean he can break the law."

Matsuzaki and Kekuchi also went out to Pupukea Ranch

to check whether Greenwell's brother, Blaine, was holding the wild pig in captivity against its will. This is also a crime. Blaine Greenwell said he let the pig go when his brother told him he was being investigated for criminal activity. "We were not going to arrest anybody," Matsuzaki said. "We just wanted to explain what the regulations are."

I asked Matsuzaki if anybody is in charge of apprehending wild pigs rooting up people's yards. He said that would be the Division of Forestry & Wildlife. State Representative Fred Hemmings, a friend of the Greenwells, said he couldn't believe the Department of Land & Natural Resources would seriously investigate the once-in-a-lifetime capture of a pig in a fish net.

"The mentality displayed in pursuing this matter, plus the time and cost involved, is so humorous it is pathetic," he said. "I would have to say the energies of the department could be better spent on matters of greater importance. If the department has any apprehension about covering their *okole* (backside) the next time somebody catches a pig in a fish net, I will volunteer as a public service to take all calls of protest."

The Great Mynah Bird Mystery

Sometimes great moments in history take place without anybody even being aware that they happened. In such a case, a little known important moment becomes a mystery. The title of this mystery is, "What Ever Happened to the Mynah Birds at the Royal Hawaiian Hotel?" This mystery has for years baffled the best minds in Hawaii as well as the entire nation like, for example, S. S. Anielski who wrote from Garfield Heights, Ohio:

"There is a book entitled *Waikiki Beachnik* by H. Allen

Smith published in 1959 which chronicles attempts to rid the Royal Hawaiian of great flocks of mynah birds which had taken up residence in trees around the hotel, keeping the guests awake." Anielski described how manager Jack Fischbeck shot off firecrackers, had the bellhops tie ropes to the tree branches and shake them, and even passed out BB guns at cocktail parties for shooting practice at the birds because they made so much noise.

The mynah birds enjoyed every minute of it and kept coming back to squabble and bicker in the tree branches every morning at dawn and every evening at sunset just when guests in the luxury hotel were trying to sleep.

Anielski wrote that on her last trip she and her husband stopped at the Royal to inquire about the mynah birds but nobody knew anything about them. She wanted to know what happened. Many people have asked the same question, especially me. Because I am the fellow H. Allen Smith stole the mynah bird story from. Actually, he didn't steal it. I traded it to him.

You see, I was a struggling young columnist when H. Allen Smith came to Waikiki to write his book. He was so prolific he could write for *Scientific American* with one hand and the *Police Gazette* with the other AT THE SAME TIME. Smith was looking for funny stories about Hawaii so I made him an offer. I would give him a very funny story about mynah birds at the Royal Hawaiian Hotel if he would write me a column about how to describe the hula for both *Playboy* and *Reader's Digest*.

He sat right down and wrote a very funny column about the hula which appeared in my first book, *Here's Hawaii*, about the same time the mynah bird story appeared in his book, *Waikiki Beachnik*. Manager Fischbeck never did get rid of the mynah birds, but he retired and Waikiki went high rise and, for some reason, the complaints about noisy mynah birds stopped.

Genial Jack Fischbeck returned for a visit in 1977 and we had a marvelous time reliving pre-statehood days at the Royal, but neither of us could figure out what happened to the mynah birds. Had the noise level in Waikiki become so high that the mynah's chatter no longer bothered guests? Was it because the windows had been sealed for air conditioning? Nobody seemed to know. Every year or so, somebody would ask, "What ever happened to the mynah birds?"

It was only by chance that I happened upon Royal Hawaiian bellman and mynah bird expert Wayne Newcomb who has worked under the Royal banyan trees since 1958. He clearly remembers Jack Fischbeck's hilarious war with the mynah birds.

"What happened to them?" I asked.

"They built the Sheraton Waikiki across the driveway in the early seventies," explained Newcomb. "When the workers went home, the crane on top of the new building hauled up all the materials for the next day. The crane swung the loads over the Chinese banyan trees where the mynah birds roosted every night. I remember those mynah birds flying up and sitting in rows on the edge of the hotel roof, grumbling at the crane.

"One morning I came to work and there were no mynah birds around. I thought, they'll come back at sundown. But the mynah birds never came back. Funny thing, they tried to move into a banyan back of Stewart's Pharmacy on the corner of Lewers and Kalakaua. But the tree was full of sparrows. There was a big war between the mynah birds and the sparrows and the mynah birds lost. I don't know where they went."

Let me hasten to assure bird lovers that they need not worry about the welfare of the homeless mynahs. As soon as my story about the missing mynah birds appeared, calls and letters began coming in about where they went. Victor Rittenband, a longtime resident of Waikiki, wrote, "I can tell you what happened to those pesky mynah birds. They are now infesting the banyan tree behind the Food Pantry on Kuhio Avenue."

Ronn Ronck, *The Advertiser's* arts writer, said the Royal mynahs moved to a banyan tree across the island in Kailua. Three readers called with inside information that the banyan tree on South Beretania Street that hangs over the parking lot of the police station is now the home of the Royal Hawaiian mynahs.

However, the strongest claim came from Louis J. Finamore, general manager of the Kahala Hilton Hotel which may be even more luxurious than the Royal Hawaiian. He said the squawking mynahs have become nonpaying guests at his inn. "If there is any way to move them back to the Royal, I would be eager to hear about it," he said.

It turned out that the Kahala Hilton mynah birds live in fiddle leaf trees that grow in the middle of a circular drive leading to the port cochere just like the banyan trees at the Royal. The trees at the Kahala Hilton are also located just under the hotel windows where the mynah birds can annoy the most people with the least effort.

"I don't know why they picked that tree in the center court," sighed manager Finamore. "We have plenty of nice trees farther from the hotel. My guess is that they like the tree because of the large leaves (about the size of paddle tennis racquets). They can get under the leaves when it rains and hide from view."

Finamore said he tried to scare the mynahs away with a supersonic siren that did no good at all. One Fourth of July some kids came around shooting firecrackers so Finamore asked the boys to throw some firecrackers into the fiddle leaf trees. "The mynah birds squawked a few times and went back to sleep," he said.

For the above reasons, I feel confident that the Royal Hawaiian mynah birds have found a comfortable home. Ask

yourself why mynah birds accustomed to luxurious accommodations at the Royal would move to the police station?

From Latrine Orderly to Millionaire

It all began in 1949 when pint-sized Shiro Matsuo was drafted into the U.S. Army and became a latrine orderly for Company B, 47th Engineers out in the pineapple fields of Apaiula beyond Haleiwa on the other side of the island from Honolulu. "I had been a clerk typist at Kodak Hawaii making $40 a month," recalled Shiro 42 years later. "At that time they didn't give Americans of Japanese ancestry rifles when we got drafted. We got menial jobs. They put me in a rock quarry at Apaiula."

"I weighed 109 pounds. The sledge hammer weighed 16. As hard as I tried, I couldn't bust one rock. The sergeant finally sent me back to camp. We AJAs were a provisional outfit assigned to the 47th Engineers. We had to do whatever the 47th told us. They made me a latrine orderly. I cleaned the toilets."

That's when a kindly mess sergeant found Shiro and rescued him from the latrine. "He took me to the kitchen," said Shiro. "He made me his yardbird. I picked out all the best portions of what he cooked and served it to the officers. It was the easiest job I ever had. We had plenty of time so he showed me how to cook and got me interested. After his unit shipped out to the South Pacific, I was assigned to another mess hall. Then I became a company cook. I was discharged as a staff sergeant in charge of a mess hall."

Shiro had found his goal in life. When he went back to civilian life he got jobs in restaurants and ended up as chef for Hawaii Governor John A. Burns at Washington Place, the governor's mansion. After that, he taught cooking at Kapiolani Community College. So many of his students opened their own restaurants that Shiro decided to go into business for himself. He took over a failing drive-in in Aiea and, within two and one-half years, had paid off $50,000 in liabilities and had sold out to buy a bigger place.

Thus was born Shiro's Saimin Haven in the Waimalu Shopping Center. Saimin is in Hawaii what hamburgers are in Omaha, Nebraska. Everybody eats saimin, a Japanese soup with Chinese noodles and a shrimp base. But Shiro was not satisfied with shrimp. He invented saimin in more flavors than there are Campbell soups. Within seven years he had branched out and was serving saimin all over the island. As a millionaire capitalist, he built a big house on a one-acre estate above Pearl Harbor. For recreation he played his concert ukulele. By all standards, the little fellow who had started as a latrine orderly had become a success.

But this was not his little known great moment in Hawaiian history. In spite of wealth and success, Shiro's life was not complete. He owed a debt to the mess cook who had taken him out of the latrine and started him on the path to fortune. Shiro's mother and father had taught him that such debts must be repaid. But the saimin king didn't know how.

"I didn't even know how to spell his name," he confessed when he came to me with his problem. "It's something like J-e-r-o-u-x. My dream has always been to repay him for what he did. Now I can say with humble pride that I'm a success and I can do it. I want to give him a two-week, all-expenses-paid vacation in Hawaii and show him around. Now that I can afford it, the thing I want most is to find this guy and thank him for teaching me how to cook."

Shiro's plea appeared on the front page of *The Advertiser* on a Saturday in January in the mid-1980s. The story was picked up by *Associated Press*, *USA Today* and the *Minneapolis Star-Tribune*. A week later Shiro received a call from Charlie Gearou, a cook in the Campus Club at the University of Minnesota. Gearou admitted that, at first, he didn't remember the 109-pound American of Japanese ancestry who worked in his kitchen when he was mess sergeant for Company B, 47th Engineers in Hawaii.

"But it all came back to me when we talked," he said. "You can imagine how surprised I was. Stunned is a better word. I really didn't try to teach Shiro how to cook. He must have looked over my shoulder and learned a lot because I understand he was a chef for one of your governors."

Gearou told Shiro over the phone that he would bring his wife to Hawaii in August when they had a vacation planned. Then he looked out of the window at the snow and decided to come in April. They flew first class as Shiro's guest on Northwest flight 21 to be greeted at Gate 13 by Shiro and a delegation of his AJA army buddies who also remembered Sgt. Gearou. Eunice, Gearou's wife, was so excited she forgot to take a single picture for the grandchildren back home. It didn't matter. There were photographers all over the place.

Shiro put his friend up at the Sheraton Waikiki, sent him to the Sheraton Maui at Kaanapali and then flew him to the Big Island of Hawaii to stay at the Sheraton Royal Waikoloa. Before Eunice and Charlie went home, Shiro invited 250 guests for a luau in their honor at his mansion on Royal Summit. There was plenty of room. His lanai will hold 400 and there's parking for 60 cars.

The Economics of Aloha

Cottage in Kahala

The impossible dream of every upwardly mobile young couple in Honolulu is a cottage in Waialae-Kahala where land is more valuable than mink or diamonds or the house you build on it. From 1950 to 1975, land in Waialae-Kahala increased in value twenty-two times. In 1975 you could buy a nice three-bedroom house a few blocks from the beach for, say, $150,000. Ten years later, the same home sold for $1 million. In 1987, an Arab businessman unloaded his beachfront Kahala estate to Japanese investors for $18 million.

These are the reasons so many people in Honolulu complain, "If only I had been smart enough to get some land when it was cheap." That's the daydream of every down-at-the-heel *kamaaina* (long time resident) who missed his chance to make a killing in real estate. One person who doesn't regret it at all is James Jay (pronounced "jeh" and meaning "thanks" in Chinese) who has lived in affluent Waialae-Kahala since 1930 when the street car didn't even go out that far.

His tenant across the street operated a chicken farm now occupied by Kahala Elementary School. Where the posh, air conditioned Kahala Mall now stands was an intersection on a country road. The business establishments located on the four corners were Joe Fatt's Barbecue, Okada's Grocery, the Nakamura Feed Store and a gas station. The shacks of Jay's former Moa Street neighbors now qualify for color photos in *House & Garden*. But he's not jealous.

So this is not the popular local fantasy of what might have been. This is a more human story of the way it really was.

"I'm a Palama boy, born and bred," said the Chinese octogenarian, longest resident of Waialae-Kahala. "When I got married they were selling house lots in Kaimuki for $200. But who can save $200 when you're raising a family on $100

a month?" He said his neighbor talked him into leasing an acre in Waialae-Kahala, a country district out past Diamond Head, at $100 a year or $8.33 per month. At the time, Jay was running a print shop.

"Two of my friends were carpenters," said Jay. "They put up my two-bedroom house for $1,000. I painted it all myself. We couldn't afford a refrigerator so we bought blocks of ice for 15 cents at the ice house back of Nakamura's Feed Store.

"We rented the rest of the land to a Japanese farmer for $100 a year and stayed there free. He had a chicken farm where Kahala School is now and there were cabbages all around. I planted fourteen mango trees and in a few years was selling mangoes to the markets downtown. On steamer day they made fruit baskets to put in the passenger cabins.

"In 1930 much of Waialae-Kahala was in kiawe trees. There were three chicken farms, three or four piggeries, one or two flower growers and two riding academies. The only paved street near me was Farmers Road. I lived on a dirt lane. The houses were mostly shacks put up by Japanese farmers. They had big families. Kids ran all over the place."

Kahala Beach was where rich people kept summer cottages as they had 100 years before in Waikiki. Torch fishermen made an exotic scene at night as they waded waist deep inside the reef spearing squid. The only time most people saw Waialae-Kahala was when they took a trip around the island by way of Waimanlo and that didn't start until the 1930s when the Territory put a road through past Makapuu Point.

Jay said his lease ran for 25 years to 1956. By that time the land owner, Bishop Estate, had developed some of Waialae-Kahala into house lots with proper roads and street lights. Jay said he was invited to take ten house lots for $800 each with an option to lease the land for about $25 a month. "I couldn't do it," he said. "Where am I gonna get $8,000?" He said contractors around town took the lots and put houses on them to sell for $14,000 to $19,000 per house.

"They couldn't give them away," said Jay. "Waialae-Kahala was too far out in the sticks and people were suspicious of leasing the land instead of buying it. I took the lot, 8,000 square feet, where I was living and moved my house on it. Finally, somebody bought a house and invited people from town to a party. All of a sudden, the houses started to sell.

"If I'd have taken those ten lots, I could be a millionaire today. But I'm not sorry. If you're too darn rich, you're not happy. I liked it better when there was more room."

Growth in Pork Butts

Economic growth in Honolulu occurs in forms not easily recognizable in other U. S. cities where communications and electronics firms are among the pace setters. It may come as a surprise, therefore, that an annual 225 percent growth rate in pork butts over a four-year period contended in the late 1980s as economic story of the year in our city. As a matter of fact, this economic indicator had never been measured before except by Judy Souza, operator services manager for Long Distance U.S.A., a local telecommunications company.

You see, Judy is one of the leading volunteers who puts on the company *luau* or Hawaiian feast every year. Last year, she had to move everything out of her freezer to get the pork butts in.

"When we started our annual Lei Day company *luau* four years ago, we had only 20 employees," she explained. "Now we've got 160. The first year, I bought five pounds of pork butts to make the *kalua* (Hawaiian style) pig. Everybody liked it. This year I had to get 50 pounds. I bought all the pork butts they had in two supermarkets. There was no more room in my freezer."

If anybody is to blame for this runaway economic expansion it is Dawn Nichols, office services manager, who talked Richard Kalbrenner, president of the company, into letting the staff throw a Lei Day *luau* in 1985. "He likes *kalua* pig," she said. "We were so small then our conference room didn't have a sink. We had to wash the dishes in the women's john down the hall and wipe everything with paper towels. The conference room only sat ten people so everybody served themselves and went back to their desks to eat."

Dawn made the *lomi* salmon (salt salmon, onions and tomatoes). "That first year, I bought five pounds of salt salmon," she said. "The second year we added squid *luau* (squid with taro tops) because the vice president in charge of technical operations is a fisherman." Memory Hanakeawe, senior billing clerk, who lives at Pearl City, pounded and salted the squid in her sink. Everybody agrees she's got the best squid *luau* recipe in the company.

But it grew so fast that Judy had to buy 12 pounds of pork butts instead of five the second year. The following year Judy shopped for 25 pounds of pork butts and Dawn bought 12 pounds of salt salmon. Her mother had to help her chop onions and tomatoes. Only squid showed no increase.

The fourth-year growth statistics are mind boggling: 50 pounds of pork butts, 16 pounds of salt salmon, 10 pounds of chicken, not to mention 60 pounds of homemade *lau laus* (pork, butterfish and taro tops wrapped in ti leaves) and 10 pounds of *poke* (raw fish and seaweed).

In spite of the drain on spare staff time, the party was a big success. Flower arrangements were stuck into the heads of cabbages. Banana stalks from Kalihi Valley decorated the empty office suite on the seventh floor of the Pacific Tower at King and Bishop Streets used as a *luau* hall. The finance department won the decorating contest with a live volcano made out of computer paper, dry ice to make smoke, and an electric fan to make the lava flow. Frankly, Judy looked a little tired after staying up until 4 A.M. two nights in a row to fix the *kalua* pig. I don't blame her.

What if the *luau* keeps growing at the same pace? My pocket calculator shows that the growth rate of *kalua* pig at Long Distance U.S.A. has been 900 percent in four years. Project that over four more years and you get 500 pounds of pork butts. Judy will have to buy nine more freezers. However, there is some hope. Kit Smith, *The Advertiser's* veteran financial writer, said, "The greatest growth of a company occurs during its early years. Tell Judy not to worry."

The Rising Cost of Kamehameha Day

Nowhere in America has the bugaboo that creates inflation, rising costs, caused more hardship than among Honolulu's *pa'u* riders. It really isn't fair. Everybody in Hawaii knows that pretty little girls who believe in fairy tales grow up to wrap themselves in ribbons and leis and twelve yards of magic skirt to become *pa'u* riders in the Kamehameha Day Parade as their grandmothers have done before them as far back as anybody can remember.

In the mid 1980s there were about 125 horses in the Kamehameha Day Parade on June 11 honoring the greatest Hawaiian of them all. Each horse bore a *pa'u* rider gowned beyond the wildest dreams of Kamehameha's *queens*. And most of the horses were rented at $250 per day. That comes to $23,500 which *pa'u* riders had to shell out for rent-a-horses.

Consider the plight of hula teacher Ellen Castillo, *pa'u* queen of the parade that year. She rode as *pa'u* marshal with her husband and with two sons as banner boys. Another son and a brother and a member of Ellen's *hula halau* (troupe) rode as outriders. "We had to rent seven horses that cost us $1,750," said Ellen.

That does not include costumes and flowers. Mary Ann Ho, the *pa'u* princess for Oahu, wore 40 strands of ilima which cost $8 a strand for a total of $320 just for flowers. "I have to spend between $700 and $800 to be Oahu princess," said Mary Ann who works as a secretary at the Pearl Harbor Naval Shipyard.

Expenses like these threaten to end the picturesque tradition of *pa'u* riding. "We had to cut back the number of *pa'u* riders for each island group in the Kamehameha Day Parade from seven to five," said Keahi Allen, past chairman of the King Kamehameha Celebration Commission. "That saved $400 to $500 for each group. If the price of horses continues to escalate, I don't know what we'll do. When I started in 1975 horses rented for $15. Now they charge $250 to $300. They say they have problems with liability and insurance."

Pa'u riding is getting to be so expensive that most women choose between the Kamehameha Day Parade and the Aloha Week Parade. That's why one of the top *pa'u* groups skipped Kamehameha Day that year. "We want to put 21 riders on horses for the Aloha Week Parade," said group member Alice Clay. "At $600 per rider, that's $12,600 minimum. Then we need five pooper scoopers to pick up what the horses leave behind. The pooper scoopers have to be color co-ordinated with the riders."

To pay for all this, the Queen's Own sponsored a benefit mixed golf tournament with an entry fee of $150 at the Pearl Country Club. All of this just for an opportunity to look as beautiful as Princess Kaiulani and as regal as Queen Emma while steering a horse. As Keahi Allen put it, "Once those girls are dressed they feel so elegant and beautiful they forget all the frustration. Even the men get more handsome."

There is more to *paʻu* riding, however, than satin and lace. B. J. Jordon, a horse owner and breeder who lives in Waimanalo, called to give us a view of the parade from under the saddle while *paʻu* riders are taking the bows. B. J. said she refuses to rent her horses to *paʻu* riders of this generation because they are better at driving cars. "Most *paʻu* riders could not possibly ride any of my horses as their horsemanship is too poor," she said.

Then there's the cost to the horse owner. In the first place, parade rules require that all horses be shod. That's $25 for shoeing. Easy Boots, rubber overshoes that won't slip and that cushion the shock of hooves on the pavement, cost another $80. We're already up to $105. In addition, any horse owner who takes pride in her animal clips and bathes him (or her) the day before the parade. "If that sounds easy, please by my guest at trying your hand(s) at bathing a 1,100-pound horse who's been rolling in Hawaiian red dirt for a month," said B. J.

She said one of her friends owns an Appaloosa whose mane stands up like a Trojan horse, so she has to set it in pink Dippity Doo rollers to make it curl. Another horse has to be equipped with a false tail because the acid in the weedy *haole koa* it grazes on makes the hair in its own tail fall out.

Now we come to the night before the parade. While the *paʻu* rider is lolling in a beautician's chair, the poor horse owner is camped out in the park with the horses because they have to be mounted and ready to go at 8 a.m. To make matters worse, the horses may not be fed on the morning of the parade because otherwise they might doo-doo all over the street. "Horse owners have to get up for a midnight feeding just so band members won't have to miss a step," B. J. sighed.

Here's her schedule for the final touch up before starting time: "Begin grooming around 6:30 a.m. or as soon as there's enough light; spot clean and scrub those white legs that got scuffed overnight. Curry, brush and polish the body; brush, comb and braid the mane and tail. Apply fly repellent, body gloss and dazzle to white areas. Paint on the hoofblack and, for heaven's sake, don't get any on those white socks you just scrubbed. Tack-up, double and triple check all equipment for flaws and wear. Wrap your poor horse in thirty to fifty pounds of leis trying to make sure no protruding wires poke or gall him. Keep him from sampling leis for taste."

B. J. said horse owners have nothing to do during the parade except race to the finish line hoping no idiot blares his horn under the horse's nose, that the horse doesn't slip on a manhole cover, that another horse doesn't kick him, or that he isn't frightened by a balloon-toting clown in a motorized hamburger. Any questions?

Fund Raising, Samoan Style

Every community devotes a portion of its economic energy to worthy causes like symphony orchestras, art museums, Little League baseball uniforms and children's theater. Honolulu is no exception. Rising young business executives are expected to collect money for the Aloha United Fund. The Punahou School Carnival, if it keeps growing, will eventually become as big as Disney World. Hawaiian churches are partial to benefit luaus, PTAs to *huli huli* (charcoal-grilled) chicken sales. The Lions Club raises money by twisting tails, the Variety Club by selling tickets and politicians by promoting $100-a-plate dinners.

It is big news, therefore, when somebody comes up with a new wrinkle in fund raising. That is what happened when the longboat owned by the village of Nuʻuuli in American Samoa broke in two after the Flag Day races at Pago Pago and High Chief Levu of Nuʻuuli went to work in Honolulu to help raise money for a new boat, thereby giving us Hawaiians a lesson in fund raising, Samoan style.

Actually, High Chief Levu's technique is not new at all. It's been used in Samoa since the first Polynesian there decided his village should have a new meeting house. However, the Samoan method may come as a breakthrough to exhausted local telephone solicitors for civic clubs and could make millionaires out of every needy soccer team in Honolulu. That's why I interviewed High Chief Levu to get the facts straight.

There happens to be a fierce competition among the Samoan villages, including arch rivals from Western Samoa, to see which longboat will win the six-mile Flag Day race every year. Similar competition among canoe clubs exists in Hawaii and it's bad enough raising money for a six-man, 40-foot-long Hawaiian racing canoe. But a Samoan longboat is to a Hawaiian canoe what a steamship is to a catamaran. "A longboat measures 90 feet from stem to stern and has 24 seats, two men to a seat," said High Chief Levu.

A fellow does nothing but sit in the bow and pound on a tin can to give the oarsmen the rhythm. One of Levu's sons is captain of the crew, another pulls an oar. Still another son is a shipfitter in Pago Pago. To make sure the new longboat is the best in the world, the village sent the shipfitter to Los Angeles to get advice from the people who built the *Stars & Stripes*, a winning America Cup yacht. The new longboat is a marvel of marine engineering, is of fiberglass instead of wood and the cost is a whopping $21,000.

As one of three high chiefs of Nu'uuli Village, Levu naturally assumed responsibility for raising some of the money. He happened to be living in the Honolulu suburb of Salt Lake at the time so went right to work here using the Samoan technique. It is called "tusiga igoa" which means "write name." Here's how it works:

First, a committee tracked down every known descendant of the village, including in-laws, everywhere in the world. They found a large contingent in California, then turned to Hawaii. The Hawaii committee consisted of High Talking Chief Seui Afa, Ioane Levu, Pi'o Lavata'i, Savaliga Leapaga, Fa'ava Savusa and Tulafono Salita. High Chief Levu said they found 200 to 300 descendants of Nu'uuli Village right here in Honolulu. On the appointed day, each Samoan on the list came to "write name," that is, to make his or her donation, write his name and be checked off by High Chief Levu himself who stayed from 6:30 A.M. to 10 P.M. to make sure nobody had an excuse for not coming.

"This list is kept," he said firmly. "It will go into the village archives. If you don't come in (and make a donation), you are cutting yourself off from the village. If I met somebody who claims to be from Nu'uuli Village and he is not on the list, I smash his face." Since High Chief Levu is also a minister of the gospel, this will give you some idea of the drawing power of Samoan fund raising.

Honest to a Vault

As we all know, the complexity of our international monetary system is built on honesty. If we did not trust one another, our credit system would collapse. Naturally we have passed laws against theft. There are sanctions against embezzlement. But, when you come right down to it, the grease that oils the ball bearings of our economy is basic human decency. That's why it is reassuring every now and then to find examples of plain, everyday people who put honor before greed.

Let's take a case in point.

Let's say, as it happened to Alesa Wilson not so long ago, that you are a teller at the Ala Moana branch of Territorial Savings & Loan. It's the end of the day. Your feet hurt. Rush hour traffic is building up. That's when you find that you've got two cents more in your cash drawer than you're supposed to have.

Imagine the dilemma! Your books HAVE to balance. That's what banks are all about. Immense sums are spent on computer systems just to make sure that the books balance. Those extra two cents could threaten the entire financial structure of Territorial Savings. It's like having your slip show. What would the other savings and loan companies say if Territorial didn't balance its books?

Seconds are ticking away. A decision has to be made. Now you've got a headache as well as sore feet. That's because you know very well what will happen when you report the two-cent surplus. Honesty is one thing. The chewing out your supervisor will give you is another matter entirely.

The two cents looms larger and larger. If you feed a surplus of two cents into the computer, an army of clerks will have to fill our forms and file them in the proper place. The computer will have to add two cents to the total cash on hand of Territorial Savings. Can you imagine the thousands of numbers that would have to be changed to make the books balance? All for two cents.

There is another alternative. You could cut a two-cent check and mail it to the customer who gave you too much in the first place. But that would require a 25-cent stamp to mail the letter, not to mention the cost of the envelope. It would cost more to mail the letter than the check is worth.

Of course, there is an easy way out. You could simply take the two cents out of the cash drawer and stick it into your pocket. That way the books would balance and your head would stop aching. Why bother the supervisor over a two-cent mistake? After all, it was the customer's fault and he's just a crusty, balding, cigar-chewing, veteran newsman who used to work at *The Advertiser* – Milt Guss. He's certainly old enough to know better and he'll never miss the two cents.

Yet, there is such a thing as honesty. And so Wilson reported the extra two cents in spite of sore feet and a headache. Now the decision became one of company policy at a much higher level. Now the reputation of Territorial Savings hung in the balance. For two cents, how many companies would care?

"It was not an easy decision," said Ala Moana branch manager Robert Abisce. "From an astute businessman's point of view, it is very inefficient to spend 25 cents to mail a two-cent check. On the other hand, the paperwork and computer time required to balance the books over two cents would be more expensive than a stamp."

That's why Guss received a check in the mail for two cents and proudly showed it around the news room. None of us had ever seen a check for two cents before. Neither had Abisce, even after 15 years in the savings and loan business. Guss said he didn't even know they owed it to him. There is only one thing that can spoil this heartwarming demonstration of honesty. Sure enough, when he goes to cash his bonanza, another more cynical teller will ask to see his ID.

The Christmas Spirit

We all know that Christmas shopping is a major economic activity that enhances the prosperity as well as the yuletide spirit of our great nation. That would be all right if only our individual contributions didn't have to cost so much. It is for this reason that I report to you how Phyllis and John C. Torres of Makaha buy Christmas presents for 20 grandchildren and eight great grandchildren without spending themselves into the poor house. They do it because John collects beer cans.

The number of beer cans Torres collects to buy his grandchildren Christmas presents should probably go down in the Guiness Book of World Records because, in 1988 alone, they weighed about 1,000 pounds. "It takes 25 Budweiser cans to make a pound," Torres explained. "Coors cans are lighter, 27 or 28 to the pound." About twice a year, Torres takes some 500 pounds of cans to the Reynolds Aluminum Recycling Convenience Center in Waianae. On the month before Christmas he took 489 pounds to the center and brought home $244.50 for the Christmas kitty.

Meanwhile, Phyllis spends the year shopping and wrapping. Her job is to buy the presents and send them off because only one grandchild lives in Hawaii. All the rest are on the Mainland. "John is almost eighty so he doesn't drive any farther than the Waianae Mall," she explained. "I catch rides with my friends when they go into town or to the Pearlridge Shopping Center. Mostly I shop at the swap meet."

Torres said he doesn't go along on the shopping excursions because his wife knows what all the kids want. The oldest grandchild at this writing was 31, the youngest 14 months. The great grandchildren are in-between.

Phyllis said the oldest gets maybe jeans, underwear or a case of beer and candy. The youngest receives a stuffed bear, clothes and a truck. "I just pick up things all year and stack 'em while John is out collecting cans," she said. "At the swap meet you can get things reasonable; aloha shirts, T-shirts, JAMS. Gee whiz, you have to look for bargains when you're buying for so many."

Torres said the tradition of a beer can Christmas in the family started when the Waianae dump was closed to scavengers. Before that he paid for Christmas presents by rescuing brass, copper and aluminum chairs from the dump and selling the metal for scrap. Collecting cans is more strenuous but it's good for him because he has a crippled leg. "When I walk, my leg comes better," he said.

He said he goes out usually after weekends and holidays when people leave cans scattered around. He parks his car and walks seven or eight miles one way and the same distance back. His favorite hunting grounds are Kaena Point, Yokohama Beach, Makua and Makaha. "John is retired but he's not the type to just sit," explained Phyllis.

Torres said he's used to working because he had to go into the fields at age eight on Kauai as a water boy on the plantation to help support the family at 20 cents a day. At age 14 he was making 10 cents an hour, a whole dollar a day for 10 hours work. Finally in 1935 he hired on with contractor Jimmy Glover for 60 cents an hour. For him, collecting beer cans is child's play and "the kids sure like to get their presents," he said.

The Economics of Auto Repair

The economics of auto repair are familiar to anybody who has ever been lucky enough to locate an honest, dependable mechanic. Once the word of this discovery gets around, the auto repairman is swamped with a tidal wave of tune-ups, slipping clutches, wheezy cylinders and defective brakes by customers who all want it fixed tomorrow for half price. The next time you take your car in, the cheerful, honest fellow who repaired it before has become a sullen, suspicious, over-worked victim of his own integrity. Can you blame him for charging what the market will bear?

This is why the hero of this tale will be known as M. G. Austin-Healey which is not his real name. At age 40, he looks like a physics professor or, say, a psychiatrist, and he has never advertised his services in the public press. That is because, as one of the best auto mechanics in Honolulu, he's afraid to.

The fellow who told me about M. G. Austin-Healey is an architect who also asked for anonymity because he owns a

Lamborghini Miura, which is one of the few cars that M. G. Austin-Healey consents to work on. Driving a Lamborghini Miura down Kapiolani Boulevard is like waving a red flag before every Nissan-Mazda-Pontiac hot rodder on the street.

"They drive up alongside and want to race," said the architect. "The only time I can drive my Miura is on Sunday." The architect owns six classic sports cars, including another Lamborghini and a Lotus, and he said he would have to send them to the mainland for repairs if M. G. Austin-Healey ever turned in his wrenches.

It is, then, a sign of our times that securing an appointment for auto repairs by a mechanic like M. G. Austin-Healey requires as much advance notice as open-heart surgery. "I've waited as long as six months for a motor job. It's a month or less for a tune-up," said the architect. "But he's concerned about doing it right. I've never run across anybody else like him in the car repair business." This is why there is a conspiracy of silence among the lucky 50 auto owners who take their cars to M. G. Austin-Healey.

He is a friendly, intellectual–looking fellow, very articulate, who said he got bored with a liberal arts major in community college because automobile engines present more of a challenge. "I get an enormous satisfaction out of taking something that isn't right and making it work," he said. "Everybody enjoys something different, and I enjoy sophisticated machinery."

He said he relies less on electronic testing than on the feel and sound of the engine to tell him what's wrong, and he works only on Italian and British cars – Ferrari, older Maseratis (no current models), Lamborghinis, selected models of Lotus and motors of historic interest.

M. G. Austin-Healey said there are no mass-produced parts for the engines he fixes. That's what makes it interesting. "You know, this kind of car is a world unto itself," he said. "There are a few people so interested in these cars that they hand-make parts to keep them going. Of course, they do it for money. But there are better ways to make money."

The mechanic said there is a network of 15 to 20 specialized auto parts shops around the country that he calls regularly from his tiny, one-man, three-stall garage in Honolulu. He has never met the people on the other end of the line but they understand each other with no effort. "Frankly, it's more efficient for me to call Pennsylvania for a part I need than to close the shop and fight traffic to a supply house in Honolulu," he said. "The parts get here in a day or two by United Parcel."

M. G. Austin-Healey said he fixes maybe two cars a week and is so absorbed in his work that he's been in the shop twelve hours a day, seven day a week, since he started. "But I'm easing up a little now," he admitted. "I'm only working eight hours on Sundays."

Hawaiian Beef Stew

One of the great dishes of the world which has never been given the respect it deserves is Hawaiian beef stew. I do not recall ever seeing this entree on the menu at the Kahala Hilton Hotel. It is spurned by such restaurants, otherwise known for excellent taste, as the Third Floor, Chez Michel and John Dominis. Fortunately, I have received instruction in the merits of this epicurean dark horse from an authority in the field. He is John Waihee, part-Hawaiian, the man elected to govern Hawaii into the 1990s. But he was merely the lowly lieutenant governor when he educated me about Hawaiian beef stew.

As I remember, we were sitting at the same table during some sort of benefit banquet in a Waikiki hotel. The subject of Hawaii's cultural complexity came up. It was then that Waihee explained his philosophy that racial relationships in the Islands can be understood by a study of Hawaiian beef stew. "You'll have to taste it to know what I mean," he said. "I'll take you around and show you. You'll see. Just don't eat breakfast first."

So it was that the great, black Lincoln Continental bearing the "State 2" license plate rolled silently up to the side entrance of the News Building. Where else but Honolulu would beef stew become a state occasion? The chauffeur drove us first to Ono's Hawaiian Food in Kapahulu. This is where U.S. Senator Dan Inouye goes for beef stew, although *lau lau* is his favorite.

Our arrival at Ono's caused a great deal of consternation because the lieutenant governor had failed to call for a reservation and we couldn't find a place to sit. In fact, nobody calls for a reservation. The place was crammed with other beef stew eaters. They were even lined up on a bench outside waiting to get in. Waihee shook hands all around, drumming up votes, until another party finished and we slipped into the booth. The lieutenant governor immediately began my education.

"We are going to three places today including this one," he said. "Each place insists they are serving Hawaiian beef stew. But it tastes different in each place. I can taste the difference between Chinese-Hawaiian, Japanese-Hawaiian, Okinawan-Hawaiian and Irish-Hawaiian beef stew. Not one recipe is exactly the same but they're all Hawaiian beef stew."

Waihee said he became a student of Hawaiian beef stew in Waimea, Hawaii where he was born, because beef stew is a ranch dish. "My father was Hawaiian-German," he explained. "He loved beef stew. We had it four times a week and each time it was different. That's because my grandmother was Chinese and my mother is a Purdy, part Irish. The stew was different each time depending on who made it."

The lieutenant governor admitted that no serious historian had yet tackled the evolution of Hawaiian beef stew nor how it became Hawaiian in the first place. "I think Hawaiians first used salt beef they got from sailing ships," Waihee said. "Today salt meat has become a delicacy among *kamaaina* ranchers." He said when he was a boy and a steer was butchered, his mother would make as much beef stew as her family could eat in several days because, once cooked, it could be reheated again and again. The remainder of the fresh meat was salted in kegs to be preserved for later use.

Stews made of this salt meat come in as many varieties as Hawaiian beef stew, Waihee said. "Hawaiians boiled it with cabbage. Then the Chinese came along and boiled it with watercress. Some Hawaiians boil it with *luau* (taro tops). All of it is known as 'salt meat.' Hawaiian beef stew is for every day, salt meat is special."

Waihee ordered a bowl of Ono's plain garden variety Hawaiian beef stew, a bowl of salt meat with watercress and a bowl of salt meat with *luau*. We dug in. Ahhhhh! The meat in the stew parted easily under a spoon. The potatoes and carrots were mealy and succulent. The reddish gravy, flavored with tomatoes, was pure ambrosia. But it was salt meat floating with watercress in a broth that tempted my palate. I had to struggle to save room for the next lesson.

This time we headed for Leong's in Kalihi, hard core Hawaiian, a favorite for entertainers. As we rolled along the freeway in air conditioned luxury, the lieutenant governor explained that Leong's has a Chinese name but it serves Hawaiian beef stew with an Irish flavor. The Lincoln Continental pulled up under a faded sign and the chauffeur opened my door. The restaurant is in the unglamorous part of town with flyspecks on the windows. We went inside to check the menu written on a blackboard.

This time there were no tomatoes in the stew. The gravy was lighter in color and had a mellow taste because of the flour. It's the Irish touch, Waihee explained. The specialty at Leong's is *luau* stew which is FANTASTIC. Waihee said he recognized a Chinese flavor of ginger from his grandmother's cooking.

He took me to one more restaurant, the Columbia Inn on Kapiolani Boulevard, for Japanese-Hawaiian beef stew. This time the gravy was brownish with a French-burgundy flavor. The meat was firmer and neatly cut into squares. Bright green peas added color. We were so full we couldn't do justice to the bowl but Waihee insisted that he likes Japanese-Hawaiian beef stew as well as the other kinds.

He said that is why Hawaiian beef stew is the great symbol of cultural integration in our town. The secret is not to worry about whether it's really Hawaiian but to learn to appreciate all the flavors that have been added by the people who came here. "We've got so much to enjoy," he said. "No one is better than the other. You take beef stew. I like one as well as the other. It didn't start out in Hawaii but Hawaiians all like it." And so does everybody else.

Chopsticks, The Confused Art

All the races of Hawaii are represented in *The Advertiser's* city room and we often eat together. It seems like every time I have Oriental food with my Japanese American friends they eat with forks while I eat with chopsticks. This is why I read with interest a story which appeared in the *New York Times* about how at least one-third of the young people in Japan are chopstick incompetents. Nobody had surveyed Hawaii diners on this important question so I went right to work.

"Just the other day this subject arose in conversation," said the Rev. Thomas Okano, a priest of the Wahiawa Hongwanji Mission. "I was visiting a member's house. Several families were there having a meal. Most of the young ones, from toddlers through high school, were using forks. Only two were using chopsticks."

Yukiko Ohara, a veteran Japanese school teacher at Waipahu Hongwanji, said her preschool-age grandchildren could not use chopsticks. "I think the younger ones today are using forks and spoons," she said.

This squared with the *New York Times* article which reported that only 48.4 per cent of the elementary school children surveyed in Japan said they could correctly use chopsticks. But Robert Iida, whose family store has been selling chopsticks for three-quarters of a century in Honolulu, said people in Hawaii are more faithful to chopsticks than people in Japan. "In Japan the trend is to break away from old customs more than in Honolulu," he said. "Here there is a desire to preserve the culture even though people do not speak Japanese. I don't see any diminished use of chopsticks here."

Jaiho Machida, the principal at the Soto Mission Japanese Language School on Nuuanu Avenue, agreed with this view. "I assume that 99 percent of Japanese Americans use chopsticks," he said. "Many people use spoon and fork but they are able to use chopsticks also."

The survey became more and more confused. Tsuneko "Scoops" Kreger, then an *Advertiser* columnist, said she had never learned to use chopsticks correctly. Eugene Kaneshiro at Columbia Inn said his nine-year-old daughter could not handle chopsticks. Dennis Ogawa, a professor of American Studies and an author of books about the Japanese community in Hawaii, confessed that he did not learn to use chopsticks correctly until he went to Japan.

It appears then, that for chopstick purposes Hawaii's population may be sorted into at least three classifications:
1. Chopstick illiterates — who don't use them at all.
2. Chopstick incompetents — who can eat with chopsticks but who hold them like ballpoint pens or darts in a pub.
3. Chopstick adepts — who wield chopsticks with grace and dexterity, holding one with thumb, fore and index finger, the other neatly tucked against the first knuckle of the ring finger.

As I suspected, there was one other chopstick complication in Honolulu that skewed the subject. While diners of Japanese ancestry may be giving up chopsticks, gourmets of other ethnic persuasions have adopted them without effort. "ALL our customers use chopsticks," insisted Lily Ota who has served Japanese food for more than 30 years at the Wisteria Cafe. "Hawaiians, Portuguese, haoles can use them as well or better than Japanese. Some Orientals more clumsy."

And the cashier, Elaine Masantai, a mere beginner at the time with only 20 years service, said the enthusiasm of other

races for chopsticks have made them more popular than ever. "These days, *haole* (white) couples demand chopsticks," she said. "You give them knife and fork and they feel insulted. We serve banquets for up to two hundred thirty people. In the buffet line are all nationalities, all get paper plates. Out of two hundred thirty, you see maybe three forks. Everybody else takes chopsticks."

Malassada Tuesday

Honolulu may be the only city in the United States which devotes a whole day to the celebration of a doughnut without a hole. This is the malassada, a mouth watering delicacy dipped in sugar that creates long lines whenever it is sold at school carnivals. Every year the Portuguese, and anybody else who is smart enough, celebrate Malassada Tuesday on the day before Lent by stuffing themselves with malassadas.

It may come as a shock, therefore, when I tell you that the malassada is the most misunderstood, mysterious, misspelled taste treat in Hawaii. Be honest. Do you know how Malassada Tuesday got started? Do you know why a delicious pastry like malassadas has a named which means "badly cooked?" I thought so.

To find out, I called Leonard's Bakery in Kapahulu, which is to the malassada what Frank Fasi is to the shaka sign. "You see, Christians used to fast during Lent, which starts on Ash Wednesday," said Margaret Rego whose late husband, Leonard, started Leonard's Bakery in 1952. "The day before Ash Wednesday is Shrove Tuesday – when everybody celebrates Mardi Gras. In England they make pancakes on Shrove Tuesday. The Portuguese make malassadas. It's the last day to feast before Lent.

"When we started the bakery, Leonard's sister-in-law said, 'Why don't you try selling malassadas on Shrove Tuesday?' She had a good recipe. So we did. It was the first time malassadas had ever been sold commercially. But the recipe was greasy. We kept changing it until we got nice, fluffy malassadas. That's all I know. Where the malassada originated, I'm not sure. We've had people from Portugal in the bakery. They never heard of malassadas."

The next authority consulted was Bernice Freitas at Kula, Maui. She's been deep frying malassadas the Tuesday before Ash Wednesday for as long as she can remember. She said she doesn't know what people in the old country ate on Shrove Tuesday but she suspects Portuguese immigrants in Hawaii were so poor all they could afford was sugar covered doughnuts. Hence, Malassada Tuesday.

Dr. A. Leslie Vasconcellos of Honolulu said he heard the reason for making malassadas on Tuesday is to use up all the flour, oil and sugar in the pantry. "These are the ingredients which would be tempting during Lent," he explained.

Ernest Morgado, vice consul for Portugal in Hawaii, said there are as many stories about the origin of malassadas as there are Portuguese. The one he believes is what his mother said her mother told her. "Malassadas came from the Azores, not Portugal," he said. "One day somebody was making a cake, my mother said. But something went wrong and the cake fell flat. Rather than throw away the dough, the cook fried it. That's how the malassada started. I believe this because the word means 'badly cooked.' I travel back to my father's village in the Azores every now and then. Last year we ordered malassadas in the hotel. They're not like here at all; very heavy and greasy and poorly cooked. Really hard to chew."

Edna Ryan, at the Hawaii Council on Portuguese Heritage, agreed with this version. She said Leonard's Bakery is responsible for teaching people besides Portuguese to eat malassadas. "But they can't spell it," she complained. "In 1979 a delegation of Portuguese went to Leonard and explained that his sign is wrong. It's spelled *malasada* instead of *malassada*. Leonard told us, 'I can't afford a new sign.' That's why everybody spells it wrong including your newspaper."

Like all Portuguese, Edna fries malassadas on Malassada Tuesday. "My mother did, now I'm doing it," she said. "It's like turkey tastes better on Thanksgiving. There's nothing like hot, fresh, malassadas on Malassada Tuesday."

A Prime Cut of Hawaiiana

Every once in a while, a story about the things we eat in Honolulu comes along that is so startling you can hardly believe it. This happened some time ago when Lester R. Walls of Haleiwa wrote in about why local beef cattle were at one time tougher on one side than the other. He insisted that wealthy *kamaainas* in bygone days ate only from the left side of the cow while plantation laborers had to make do with the tougher right side.

Walls went on to explain the tender left side was known as uphill beef while the tough right side was called downhill beef in Hawaii. Here's why. After Captain George Vancouver introduced cattle to the Islands in the 1790s, King Kamehameha put a *kapu* on them so they would multiply. These cattle grazed on the slopes of Mauna Kea. Being in the northern hemisphere, they grazed around the mountain in a counterclockwise direction the way water spins when it is going down the drain.

As a result, the right legs of the cattle had to take longer steps than the left legs because the right legs were on the downhill side. This went on for decade after decade on the open, unfenced range. *Kamaainas* eventually discovered that the downhill, longer stepping quarters of Island beef were tougher and that the prime cuts came from the uphill portions. In time, it became a status symbol to eat beef from the left side which was, of course, their right. Only the wealthy could afford it. This had a heavy social and economic impact, Walls reported.

I'll bet you never knew that.

Anyway, there were so many "beefs" from the poor people about eating from the right side that the government took the matter under consideration. They put to work the experts who had imported mongooses in Hawaii to eat the rats and ended up with both rats and mongooses. After much study, the experts discovered that Argentine cattle, living in the Southern Hemisphere, graze in a clockwise direction because, as in Hawaii, there are a lot of hills in Argentina.

Naturally, the legs on the left side of the Argentine cows have to take longer steps than the right as they graze around a hill. Therefore, they become stringy and tough, just the opposite of Hawaii. Lengthy, secret negotiations to breed downhill Hawaiian with uphill Argentine cattle to produce uniformly tender Hawaiiantine steaks were nearly complete when World War II broke out. The resulting population explosion caused the importation of beef from the Mainland and the fencing of the Islands for military reservations.

Cattle could no longer graze very far in any direction, counterclockwise or wherever. And so you no longer have to worry about uphill and downhill when you order beef in a restaurant. Our thanks go to Mr. Walls of Haleiwa for passing on this little known gem of Hawaiiana. In fact, it's so little known I have not been able to find a single person in the cattle industry who ever heard of it before.

One–Ton Style Sushi

The preparation of food to celebrate the holiday season is a ritual honored throughout our great nation in kitchens from Portland, Oregon to Portland, Maine where household cooks rush around mashing potatoes, roasting turkeys and baking apple pies. This ritual is apt to take a somewhat different turn in Hawaii where a lot of people prefer rice cakes to apple pie and s*ushi* (rice balls) to mashed potatoes, and they eat to celebrate the New Year, not Christmas. As a result, one of the wildest New Year's parties in Honolulu takes place not in Waikiki nightclubs but in the kitchen of Fukuya, the 50-year-old Japanese family delicatessen in Moiliili.

By 6 p.m. on December 31 the holiday hungry of Honolulu annually cart away about 3,000 *maki nori* (rolls of *sushi* wrapped in seaweed), 2,000 *inari* (cone *sushi* with *tofu* shells) and about 1,000 pounds of *mochi* (fancy rice cakes). "It's a madhouse every year," said Ed Iwahiro who, with his wife, Lorna, her mother, sister, two uncles, family friends and assorted helpers process a ton of rice to fill holiday orders.

It's all done by hand. I timed Elsie Sasaki while she rolled *maki nori* in a flexible mat made of bamboo slivers. It took her a minute and twenty seconds to fill one *sushi* and roll it. She said she can do twenty in half an hour. Lorna, the fastest *sushi* slinger in the west, can stuff a cone of *tofu* with rice for *inari* in five seconds.

But that's only the tip of the iceberg. Shopping for the ingredients, and washing and slicing and cooking them is like filling a supply order for the Normandy invasion. Start with 20 bags of rice at 200 pounds each. For the *sushi* you also need carrots, string beans, *age* (the *tofu* shells for cone *sushi*), canned tuna, *campyo* (dried squash), *kamaboko* (fish cake) and eight hundred eggs. Meanwhile, the New Year's orders for *sushi* and *mochi* have been coming in for a month.

On December 30, Lorna and Ed with half a dozen helpers come to work at 5 A.M. They knock off at 3 P.M., then come back at 7 P.M. for an all night effort. It starts with washing and cutting. And frying eggs. The 800 eggs have to be fried individually in square skillets which produce sheets of fried eggs of the size needed for wrapping *maki*. Ed said one woman does nothing but fry eggs.

By 11 P.M. the family begins boiling the string beans and carrots, and cooking the rice and tuna. That's in the kitchen. Meanwhile, back in the *mochi* room, old Mr. Yamada, who sold his business to Ed and Lorna, is supervising his own ten helpers. The rice is first washed, then soaked before it's cooked. Wayne Yoshikawa, a carpet layer and friend of Ed's, helps wash the rice. After the *mochi* rice is cooked, it's scooped ten pounds at a time into the mechanical *mochi* pounder. The rice comes out like dough which is separated by hand into little cakes. Vieng Khamvongsa from Laos packs *mochi* cakes for delivery.

Back in the kitchen, family friends, relatives and other part-time helpers arrive at 3 A.M. to start rolling, sorting and packing *sushi*. Jill, Lorna's sister, normally displays it on fancy plates in attractive designs. "But there isn't time on New Year's even to cut the rolls into individual *sushi*," she sighed. "We're too busy rolling."

By the time it's light on New Year's Eve day, customers are lining up for their orders. Two workers frantically sort *sushi* and five more box it. Sometimes the line goes way out to the parking lot. By 7 P.M. on New Year's Eve day the rush is finally over, the kitchen is cleaned and the front door locked. Ed said Lorna goes straight home to bed and he goes out to have a drink.

Ethnic Free Lunch & Legislative Opening

Long before Captain Cook messed everything up, the old Hawaiians established such sensible customs as the *makahiki*, a time of the year between December and February when war was forbidden and rulers received homage in return for putting on feasts and hula entertainment for their subjects. Fortunately this delightful institution has survived in modern form as the annual Ethnic Free Lunch & Legislative Opening along about the middle of January in the State Capitol.

On the opening day of the legislature, our law makers greet each other effusively like delegates to a class reunion, make complimentary speeches and graciously postpone warfare for twenty-four hours. At this opening session, hula dancers perform in the chambers of both the house and the senate while the legislators are adorned with leis. The important business of the day comes at noon when the senators and representatives serve lunch in their offices to people who may or may not have voted for them.

It is by far the best free lunch in town and the menu is dazzling. I have reported on this feast for about fifteen years and am considered an authority. Quite a number of memorable dishes stand out in my mind. For example, in 1987 Representative Ron Menor's uncle, Andy, brought a 110-pound pig roasted Filipino style. He just happened to have the recipe in his pocket so here it is:

Dress the pig and rub it down with salt. Inside the pig you stuff spices – bay leaf, garlic, black pepper, lemon leaf, ajinomoto and a little bit of vinegar. Next you stitch up the belly, put the pig on a spit and roast it over *kiawe* charcoal for eight hours. This pig was prepared the night before in Waialua by Lita Mabini's family. The meat was very tender and juicy and the spices gave it more flavor than *kalua* pig.

In 1986 Representative Richard Kawakami's mother on

Kauai introduced stuffed cuttlefish. She said she chops up the tentacles with bacon, stuffs it into the body of the cuttlefish, wraps it in tinfoil and bakes it. Cut into thin slices, it is tender and delicious with a faint bacon-fish flavor.

Probably the biggest breakthrough in ethnic legislative food came in the early 1980s when the parents of Representative Calvin Say served a stew of pigs' intestines in a huge, silver warming bowl. This Hawaiian dish is called *na'au* and I can't say that it is my favorite although the line reached clear out into the hall. The Says scored another triumph by serving chicken feet, a Filipino dish you won't find in restaurants.

Among the outstanding dishes in my memory is the baked salmon served annually by Senator Milton Holt. His mother, Frances, goes fishing in Alaska every year and brings home enough salmon to fill the senator's deep freeze. For legislative openings and fund raisers, his father bakes the fish with chopped onions, celery, spices and mayonnaise topping. It comes out light, moist and tender with a delicate flavor.

One other dish captured my taste buds in 1990, Representative Paul Oshiro's cucumber (Korean) *kim chee*. That cucumber – prepared by Oshiro's auntie, Pat Nagamine of Ewa Beach – makes a dill pickle taste like a soggy bagel.

Some of the legislators have slacked off on their menus because of high food prices and the fact that they are feeding people that never voted for them. There is even talk of discontinuing the Legislative Ethnic Free Lunch. For example, Representative Mike Crozier, who serves ice cream, was greeted by an enthusiastic free loader who shook his hand and said, "Congratulations on your election, Mr. Haagen-Dazs." But law makers and their campaign volunteers continue to exhibit the aloha spirit. A school teacher, a medical assistant, an airline sales clerk, a housewife, a high school counselor and a police officer worked all night to prepare the dishes served by House Speaker Daniel Kihano in 1988. "We don't care who eats our food," said one of the volunteers. "Mrs. Kihano

feels if you're hungry, come in. If the food runs out, it runs out. This isn't a taking day, it's a giving day."

I must confess, however, that 1989 almost sunk me. My first mistake was to try Auntie Elvie's *halo halo* (a Filipino coconut pick-me-up) before sinking my teeth into Willie Kaupiko's home-dried Waianae *opelu* (Hawaiian mackerel). Then I couldn't resist the *poke* (seaweed and raw fish) at Representative Sam Lee's office while still trying to digest the coconut and bean *manju* (Japanese pastry) that Representative Joe Souki brought over from Maui. My downfall came at Representative Karen Horita's seafood restaurant. She served crab, clams, *nigiri sushi* (rice balls) from a *sushi* bar, *poke* and two kinds of *sashimi* (raw fish). The desserts were in the next room – chocolate squares with thick frosting, cheesecake with fruit topping and French pastries.

I could only hope that all of the above went with Representative Mike Crozier's macadamia nut ice cream. If it didn't somebody was going to be in trouble.

Dining At The Fire Station

Veteran firefighter Lee Muller still recalls his most terrifying moment after donning the uniform and joining the brave crew at the Kuakini Fire Station. Was it battling a dangerous blaze? Scaling a spider web ladder to dizzy heights above the street? Nope. It was cooking for the first time for the hungry and discriminating members of his watch.

"I'd say that is the worst fear of a new recruit," Muller confessed. "At a big station, you have to take your turn at cooking for 12 to 14 men. It's overwhelming. I'm probably the only fireman in Hawaii who ever burned the spaghetti noodles while boiling them. I still can't figure out how I did it. They kidded me about it for months."

Now, after about a decade of trial by fire, Muller is an excellent cook. The week before I talked to him he served up fried chicken with sweet sour sauce and roast pork as entrees, rice and salad on the side. And he doesn't consider himself unusual.

"Most of the men on my watch cook better than I do," he said. "I look forward to coming to the station because I eat better here than at home. All the single guys are like that and a lot of the married men. I'd say most firemen cook better than their wives."

Debbie Wayman, who started as a firefighter at the Kuakini Station about a year ago, isn't about to disagree. She said the biggest worry of her recruit class was not about new apparatus or where they were being assigned, but what the other firefighters would say about their cooking. "The Fire Department is known for good food," she explained. "At home my husband and I just fix something fast. Here at the station it has to be GOOD and you have to cook plenty of it."

There has never been a contest to determine which of the forty fire stations on Oahu serves the best food or which firefighter is the best cook. But there are some outstanding candidates.

For example, Herbert Ho at the Kahuku Station is such an accomplished chef that he operates a family catering business in his spare time. Kahuku firefighters are such good cooks they prepare a feast for the Kahuku High School football team before every game.

The Kailua Station is noted not only for its chefs but also for a baker, Lloyd Wright, who whips up apple and banana pies, bread puddings or pineapple upside-down cakes for his watch. At Central Fire Station, Nathan Kapule is a whiz at banana bread.

There seems to be no limit to the ingenuity of firefighters as cooks. Glenn Sato at the Waialua Station gets his inspiration from Shilling spice labels. "There's a different suggestion on each spice label about what to cook with it," said Sato. "That's what got me started. I'd see what menus fit and learned to cook 'em. Now I can make about 30 different dishes."

Muller admitted that he gets a lot of his ideas from senior citizen ladies of all races in the supermarket. "The man who does the cooking that day has to do the shopping," he explained. "We can spend only $4.50 (allotted by the department) per man so we go for what's on special. Ladies are always looking into my cart and asking me what I'm going to cook. When I tell them, they give me different ideas."

Bob Thomas of Hawaii Kai Fire Station serves an economical luncheon surprise, cole slaw with chili. "It's good mixed together," he insists. "The mayonnaise and chili are a perfect combination." The recipes are gathered in Peter O'Sullivan's *Firefighters of Hawaii Cookbook* available at most book stores.

Firefighters' Menu
SUNDAY – (Kahuku Fire Station) *Miso* soup, fresh aku (tuna) *sashimi*, *aku* tempura, fried chicken, meat loaf, rice, green salad.

MONDAY – (Central Fire Station) Chicken *harm ha* (Vietnamese style), ginger chicken, stir-fry noodles, rice, salad.

TUESDAY – (Kaaawa Fire Station) Chicken egg plant stir fry, potato salad, rice.

WEDNESDAY – (Hawaii Kai Fire Station) Swiss steak, shoyu chicken, chicken sukiyaki, cole slaw, rice.

THURSDAY – (Waialua Fire Station) Chicken adobo (Filipino style), green salad with alfalfa sprouts, rice.

FRIDAY – (Kuakini Fire Station) Roast chicken with duck sauce, baked pork chops with sugar/tomato/sliced lemon, tossed green salad, rice.

SATURDAY – (Kailua Fire Station) Chicken stew with Portuguese sausage, meat loaf, cole slaw, rice, pineapple upside-down cake.

Prince of the Beach Boys

The royal families of Hawaii, as in most modern countries, no longer hold the autocratic power they once did though there are a few princely old timers who still portray the role of nobility. So it is with Joe Akana, last active member of Waikiki Beach Royalty, Ohua Lane Dynasty, who once ruled the Moana Hotel Pier among the maharajas, millionaires and movie stars.

Joe was dubbed to the nobility by Dudey Miller, the first king of the beach boys. You may not have heard about Dudey Miller because Duke Kahanamoku usurped his throne by breaking three world swimming records at the Olympic Games in Stockholm, Sweden in 1912. Also, Duke was descended from the better known Kalia line of Waikiki nobility, down where the Hilton Hawaiian Village is now. Joe Akana and Dudey Miller came from the Ohua Lane line, closely allied with the Paokalani and Kapahulu dynasties on the Diamond Head side of Kuhio Beach. This story concerns the Ohua Lane line of beach boys about which little was known until Joe placed himself in the koa rocking chair in my office and opened the archives of his memory.

The Ohua Lane kingdom was a colorful place inhabited by Hawaiians including Old Man Kaloa, the turnkey at Oahu Prison, who wore tails and a derby hat to work on the electric trolley every morning when Joe was a youngster. "It is important to mention Johnny Kia Nahauelelua," said Joe. "He was head fisherman on Ohua Lane. He had seven or eight fishermen under his command. They fished from canoes, later from row boats. They delivered their fish in baskets on the trolley to the Kekauliki Fish Market downtown. Whoever made the sale would come back with a demijohn of wine."

The warriors of Ohua Lane were members of the Stone-wall Gang, so called because they sat in the evening and played music on the stone wall below Kuhio Beach. People parked their cars and listened. When Joe was in the first grade in 1913, Queen Liliuokalani passed by in her hack every day at 5 P.M. Boys on the stone wall would stand up and bow. The queen would lean out of the hack and smile. The Stonewall Gang did battle in barefoot football with Kalihi's Thundering Herd and various other armies from Palama, School Street, Moiliili, Kaimuki, etc.

Kakaako also had a gang which monopolized coin diving in Honolulu Harbor when ocean liners came to town. "They did not like anybody else to break in," said Joe. "If they didn't know you, they'd stick their fingers in your eyes when you went down for a coin." However, an Ohua Lane warrior named Hard Head Harvey did manage to penetrate the Kakaako defenses because of his thick skull. His head was so hard that he could swan dive off the crow's nest. But only if the collection was big enough. This was while Joe attended high school just after World War I.

While the Kakaako kids dived for coins, the boys from Ohua Lane headed for Waikiki Beach to study the duties and responsibilities of the beach boy nobility. "Every time an around-the-world liner came in I played hooky from school and went to the beach," Joe explained. "I'd hang around, try to be second captain in a canoe or give a surfing lesson or two. Those passenger ships would stay overnight, sometimes two or three days. If you had a good day, you could make $15. You could make at least $6 or $7 anytime."

So Joe was trained for the nobility. He joined the Hui Nalu Beach Club and, although he weighed only 135 pounds, handled himself well in combat. This was important for the Hui Nalu boys sometimes waged war. Joe said he was told of the legendary battle in the olden days between Hui Nalu and the crew of the *Great Northern*, an ocean liner, which took place somewhere in Waikiki. Alas, the Hui Nalu army was outweighed and caught by surprise. They got clobbered. Hui Nalu went into training. The next time the *Great Northern* came into port, they were ready. They got clobbered again. Ah well, you can't win 'em all.

After a proper period of apprenticeship, such a warrior as Joe Akana might become a full-fledged knight of the surfboard, eligible to play his ukulele on the Moana Hotel pier on Sunday nights with the other beach boys. So it happened in the early 1920s when Joe took over management of Dudey Miller's Moana Beach concession from Hiram Anahu, composer and artist and graduate of Kamehameha School. The beach boy dynasties were then in full flower. Through the 1930s, wealthy tourists often stayed at the Royal Hawaiian Hotel for a month or more every year. Each beach boy had his regular clients and became a trusted member of the family.

Joe said he took care of the Michels family, heir to a drug fortune. They had three boys whose ages ranged from twelve on up. Beach boys took such charges to the movies barefooted and taught them to eat saimin. "One year the volcano erupted," Joe said. "The Michels boys came and said their parents would let them go to see the eruption if I took them. We went on the steamer and had a very good time. The last year they were here, the oldest boy, Henry, brought his Pierce Arrow and we'd ride around in it blowing the fog horn."

Joe said his richest client was the Maharaja of Indor who brought both of his Bentleys to Hawaii. Also a staff of seventeen in addition to his wife. "He was 28 years old and his wife was 24," said Joe. "None of his staff was allowed to ride in the elevator with him or in his cars. But I could. I was given the permission to cash any amount I needed in his name to pay for entertainment of his staff. Before he left, his secretary passed out envelopes with very generous tips to everybody who had anything to do with his stay here. He sent me on a trip to California."

Wealth and romance were daily ingredients in a beach boy's life, Joe said, and he enjoyed it thoroughly. But there were also hazards. One year an impresario named Danny O'Shea brought his dance troupe to the Princess Theater. The chorus girls cut a wide swath among Waikiki's beach boys. Carnegie Wilcox fell in love with one of them. Hiram Anahu married another. Joe's brother took still another for his wife. Carnegie got divorced. Hiram and his wife were happy together. But Joe's brother put a bullet through his head over the woman he married.

"The member of a prominent family got involved with her," said Joe. "But his family pulled him back. She got involved with another man and he tried to end his life but his family watched him too close. Then there was a famous athlete who took poison over her. Finally, another well-known man tried to commit suicide over her but he came out of it. The woman was not beautiful. She was a little too plump. But she was a humdinger. These things happened in the beach crowd. If you could hear some of the stories..."

Other members of the royal families have all gone to that great surf spot in the sky. Panama Dave died of drink. Chick Daniels is no more. Charlie Amalu went to a nursing home. Duck has gone to his honorable reward. Joe said he was more fortunate than the other colorful characters who made their living on the beach. He had a back-up skill. As a mortician, he still held the 24th embalmer's license issued in Hawaii.

Princess Pupule and Her Papayas

We have heard from a male member of Hawaiian royalty. Now it is time to reflect on the female side which provides a somewhat different view of events in the lives of the nobility. The opportunity to do this came in the mid-1980s when Carmen Joyce, an unsung Honolulu legend, the Auntie Mame of old Waikiki, a member of the dance troupe which broke so many hearts on the beach, arrived in our city from California for a visit.

The blood pressures of quite a few kamaaina, white-haired gentlemen may have gone up somewhat when they read in *The Advertiser* that Carmen was in town. You may ask your grandfather why. Better still, ask your grandmother. If they won't tell you, I will.

Carmen Joyce cut a swath through the local male population that made beach boys shake their heads in awe. "Princess Pupule," the popular song, was written about Carmen, the girl who had plenty papaya and loved to give them away. She ended up as a mere beauty operator, but men lost their hearts to her like flowers lose their petals. Carmen said she couldn't remember whether she was married four or five times. But she could recall the price of a lease in old Kahala as if it were yesterday. She didn't regret a moment.

"Sometimes when I look in the mirror, I think I should go in for a face lift," she said as she lit another filter-tip cigaret. "Then I tell myself, 'Who am I going to fool?' I'd rather buy another bottle of scotch."

Carmen was not sure at first whether she should confide in a callow youth like me. After all, beauty operators are privy to information that never gets in the news. Her customers included Mrs. Walter Dillingham for whom La Pietra was built as a honeymoon cottage; Mrs. Lester McCoy, the art patron for whose husband McCoy Pavilion in Ala Moana Park is named; Mrs. Stanley Kennedy, whose husband founded Hawaiian Airlines. Then there were the Rices, Cookes, Athertons and lots more.

This, then, is the story of a single girl, extraordinarily beautiful, who came to Honolulu at age twenty-six in 1924

after dancing in the chorus line of the Ziegfeld Follies for five years. "I came here in a show that was booked for six weeks at the Princess Theater," said Carmen. "We had 16 girls. It was a small show by mainland standards. I had some singing parts and was paid $50 a week." Carmen said she earned more in New York but she wanted to see Hawaii and this was a way to do that.

"I came from a poor family so I always had to work my way," she explained. "The show played for ten weeks instead of six and, by that time, I had fallen in love with the place. It was so colorful and fascinating to me. On Fort Street you would see Chinese women with bound feet, Japanese women in kimonos, Hawaiians in muumuus and leis, and men in their white suits. A policeman sat under an umbrella at one of the downtown intersections. He operated the stop-and-go signal. After he got back from lunch he would fall asleep. Drivers would stop and laugh. If he didn't wake up, they'd honk."

Carmen said she had had a bit of beauty parlor experience so she got a job as a beauty operator downtown at $25 a week. Her first customer was Louise Dillingham, wife of Walter F. Dillingham, head of the Dillingham empire. It was Louise Dillingham who urged Carmen to open her own shop and found her a place across from McInerny's at Fort and Merchant Streets. Carmen said she started very small, hiring only one girl at a time. Soon the most important women in Honolulu were stopping for permanent waves.

"My customers invited me to their parties," said Carmen. "But I quit going. I was young and cute and the husbands tried to...I had been in show business and knew all about that. I wanted nothing to do with somebody else's husband." This may have solidified her position with her elite clientele. Carmen said they liked her because she was independent and energetic and full of life. At Christmas her wealthy customers gave her beautiful gifts.

"After a while, they got tired of giving me clothes and

jewelry and began giving me stock," she said. "Mrs. Stanley Kennedy started it with stock in her husband's new airline. I got C. Brewer stock and Dillingham stock. It became quite valuable. That's what is keeping me today. One of my customers told me about lease land at Kahala. She said, 'You'll make money, Carmen.' I leased two lots for 50 years at $100 a year, then built a house on one lot and sold the other lease a few years later for several thousand dollars."

Carmen said her first husband was a beach boy whom she divorced. He committed suicide which, she said, might have been due to drinking. Others say it was over her. The scion of a very prominent family fell in love with her. "We were young," she said. "He took me dancing, on dates. He wanted to marry me and told his mother. She called me and offered me money to give him up. I told her I wasn't that kind of a woman. I don't think I would have married him anyway. He was a real wild Indian when he drank. I refused to ride in a car with him."

She said the social center for her friends was the old Outrigger Club between the Moana and Royal Hawaiian Hotels where everybody went for a swim after getting off work at 4 P.M. "The beach boys began calling me 'Princess Pupule,'" said Carmen. "One night at a party in the Haleiwa Hotel we were drinking and clowning around. Somebody wanted a papaya. I had a friend across the way so I got some and passed them around. A fellow named Reynolds wrote that song, *Princess Pupule*, about it."

By this time Carmen had opened another beauty shop in Waikiki. She remembers the Massie Case in the 1930s. After the alleged rape of Thalia Massie, her mother, Mrs. Grace Fortesque, the matriarch of a prominent East Coast family, came to Hawaii and Carmen did her hair. "Women went to the beauty parlor once a week in those days," Carmen explained. "Mrs. Fortesque was a horrible old woman. The daughter was very nice but I don't think I ever did her hair.

They never did get that case straightened out but it sure had Honolulu in an uproar. They asked women not to go downtown alone at night. The FBI came around and asked me not to discuss the case in the beauty parlor."

Carmen married and divorced two more husbands before World War II. Since she was single at the time, she enlisted in the WAC and was sent to the South Pacific where she served as a file clerk in New Guinea and Leyte. "I was in for four years," she said. "I came out a lieutenant. General Mark Clark commissioned me. I knew him. He rented my house in Kahala. Later I was standing at attention in the Philippines. He said, 'Carmen, what the hell are you doing here?' I said, 'Well, sir, I suppose the same thing you are.'"

Grampa Is My Press Agent

Hawaii is not a good place to watch for important people, even though there are plenty around, because you can't tell them from anybody else. Hardly any male except an attorney in court wears a coat and tie anymore. It is true that females in business are dressing up and that panty hose have become the symbol of success among professional women. But on the beach you can't distinguish between a female executive vice president and a cocktail waitress.

Nevertheless, there is a growing awareness about who we are and how we got here. Every year you find more people in the State Archives looking up their ancestors. By this time every Hawaiian in town is descended from an important chief while the Japanese prefer samurai ancestry. In 1986 veteran show business promoter Kimo Wilder McVay broke new ground in the science of genealogy when he discovered a new star – his two-month-old granddaughter.

The little girl's name is Ryan Kinau Mateo. At the time, she was in Honolulu with her parents from Hacienda Heights, California to visit relatives. Even before she was born, Kimo developed an interest in her roots. It was only natural to expect great things from his research. After all, McVay has promoted singer Don Ho, surfing legend Duke Kahanamoku, Polynesian review impresario Tavana, standup comic Andy Bumatai and pro footballer Russ Francis. So he applied the same techniques of ballyhoo to his granddaughter's billing. By the time Ryan was born, he had her related to Robin Hood, Kamehameha the Great and the man who started the Pony Express. Kimo is especially proud to have dug Robin Hood out of his granddaughter's closet. "Everybody has a thief in the family," he said. "You might as well have one with class."

Other grandfathers pull photos from their wallets as an excuse to talk about their offspring. Kimo carries around a file of clippings and family trees to prove that Ryan's ancestors came over on the Mayflower, discovered Hawaii and played key roles in the Philippines and China.

One word of caution may be in order here. Kimo, who began his career in a piano bar, may still have a few things to learn about history. This reporter expressed interest in the fact that one of Kimo's granddaughter's ancestors was Roger Williams of early American colonial fame.

"I feel the same way," said Kimo. "It was a surprise to find out that we are related to such a famous piano player," said Kimo.

"No, this Roger Williams founded the colony of Rhode Island," I explained.

The information about Roger Williams, as well as that about Robin Hood, comes from a letter written by Kimo's grandfather, James Austin (Kimo) Wilder, to Kimo's brother: "You are the great-great-great godson of Kamehameha the First by reason of the adoption or *malu* by Queen Kinau (of a Wilder ancestor). You are related to hundreds of New England families; Judd, Fish, Williams (Roger), Hastings (Earl Huntington or Robin Hood)."

Kimo explained casually with a flick of cigarette ash that his grandfather was the first person to play the ukulele on stage in the U.S. while Hawaii was an independent monarchy. "That was in 1889 at Harvard," said Kimo. "He was a member of the Hasty Pudding Club and a fraternity brother of Franklin D. Roosevelt who, when he was secretary of the Navy, helped him found the Sea Scouts of America."

Kimo explained that one of the things that got him interested in his roots is his son-in-law, Jodi Naumu Mateo, whose father is Filipino and his mother Chinese-Hawaiian. Historians are now eagerly awaiting to see what a genius in the art of razzle dazzle will be able to do with this familiar Island genealogical material. Kimo has already discovered two football stars and a professional wrestler.

Oh yes, about the Pony Express. "There are great similarities among several branches of the families," Kimo said. "My great-grandfather, S.G. Wilder, founded the Wilder Steamship Co. in Hawaii. My grandfather married a Harnden. William Harnden founded the express business in the United States (of which the Pony Express was a part) in the 1840s." Little Ryan made no comment. She seemed content to snuggle in her blankets and let her grandfather handle her promotion.

Tony Lee, Korean Horatio Alger

One reason it is smart to be polite to people who look unimportant in Hawaii is because you never know when they'll buy the company you work for. This is especially true of immigrants who don't seem to understand that the days of Horatio Alger are supposed to be over. Take Tony Lee, the watchmaker at Swiss Watch Repair on upper Kalakaua Avenue. He isn't Swiss. Tony has never been near Switzerland. He emigrated from Korea in 1973. But that doesn't make him Korean, either.

What Tony Lee IS drove Columbus to the New World, sent pioneers across the plains and put humans in space. The way Tony Lee has overcome bad luck makes Horatio Alger look like a yuppie.

At age fifteen he had never ridden in a car. His family was too poor even to own a bicycle. In the shambles of postwar Korea, Tony Lee apprenticed himself to a barber. He swept the floor, cleaned windows and washed hair in exchange for one meal a day. While scrubbing the floor, he spilled some water on the barber's shoes. The barber kicked him in the face and bloodied his nose.

Disenchanted with barbering, Tony talked his father into selling enough rice to send him to watchmaking school. But the money ran out before graduation. Therefore, Tony could not get a job as watchmaker. He and a young friend who was learning to be a barber set out on foot, like New England tin peddlers, to cut hair and fix watches in the villages. The two teenagers starved and shivered unless they found a funeral with free food. After a couple of months, Tony came down with pneumonia and went home. But he had fixed enough watches to earn $200, all of which went for medicine.

Then Tony stayed with a friend who operated a comic book stall on the street, six by six feet. They both slept there until Tony landed a job in a jewelry store. The owner fed him. In return, Tony ran errands and cleaned up the place. He also got to fix watches and learned a lot.

About this time, his luck turned. His father sold some land and helped him open his own watchmaking stall near Kimpo International Airport. Thus, at age sixteen, Tony

became a capitalist. He learned the business fast and money began rolling in. Soon Tony hired assistants. In time, he got married. He taught seven of his relatives to fix watches. Each opened his own shop and began making money. In 1987 one of these relatives put up his own high-rise the size of Century Center in Korea across the street from Tony's shop.

It was a brother-in-law who talked Tony into coming to the U.S. He arrived in Hawaii with a wife and child and $800. They stayed with a sister in Pearl City. Nobody would give him a job as watchmaker because they couldn't understand him. He didn't speak English. So he worked as a busboy, janitor, delivery man, car polisher. Every month, $50 went home to his parents.

Finally he sold his car for a plane ticket to Washington, D.C. where he had a friend. There he was hired at an Omega watch outlet where he repaired watches while learning English. Meanwhile, he rented a two-bedroom apartment and rented out one of the bedrooms. In two years, he saved enough to bring his parents from Korea and his family from Hawaii.

From Washington, they moved to Virginia where Tony bought a $60,000 house on the Potomac. But he didn't like the crime in that part of the country. His sister wrote that there isn't much crime in Hawaii. The Lees moved back in 1978. Tony immediately lost his savings in a bad investment. He drove a taxi 18 hours a day until he'd saved enough to open a hole-in-the-wall watch repair place in Kapahulu.

It did so well he moved to upper Waikiki two years ago. After work, he makes house calls to fix grandfather clocks all over the island. He has three children now. His parents still live with him. "Very happiness to work," he said. "For me, nothing impossible. People bring watch frozen with rust. I losing time to fix. I don't care. It's happiness work. For me, nothing impossible to repair watch."

Birds of a Feather

Not all of our important visitors come to Hawaii on commercial airlines or by ship. Some of our most discriminating tourists fly themselves from Alaska to spend the winter. They are known as golden plover, birds of an unusual feather, who arrive in August and stay until the following spring when they fly back to mate and hatch babies. While in Hawaii they camp out on the best real estate; exclusive golf courses, lawns of the rich and famous, and the grounds of Iolani Palace.

In 1987 I took the first survey of how many golden plover make reservations for our finest lawns. The figures show that up to eleven golden plover took up winter residence at Iolani Palace. Eight more camped out at Honolulu Hale (City Hall) and six at the State Capitol. Kawaiahao Church supported five and the Neal Blaisdell Center five more. These statistics had never before been released to the public, not even by the Hawaii Visitors Bureau.

Yet every year the same birds fly 2,000 miles to spend the winter at Iolani Place. The same eight go to City Hall, the same six to the Capitol, the same five to Kawaiahao Church. What's more, each bird returns to its own section of lawn.

Even the Sheraton chain doesn't have a reservations system as efficient as that. Such sophistication makes our State Bird, the nene, look like a dumb goose. After all, the only reason the nene ended up in Hawaii from its home in Canada was because it got lost. Once the nene got here, it couldn't find its way back and so it eventually became the State Bird.

Dr. Phil Bruner, assistant professor of biology at Brigham Young University-Hawaii, has studied plover for about a decade. He said he is amazed at their ability to navigate here over open ocean. "Presumably they use both sun and star compasses," he said. "There is some evidence they can sense magnetic north. They fly too high to use swells for direction, probably at about 20,000 feet where there is little turbulence and above the clouds for celestial navigation."

Bruner said there are no headwinds up that high. In fact, the plover may pick up the jet stream. "The cost of flying at that altitude is heat loss," he explained. "It takes them a minimum of 56 hours (to fly 2,000 miles at an average speed of 35.7 miles per hour) but they must have fat reserve for 78 hours."

These figures seem incredible when you watch the dainty little birds tiptoeing across the Iolani Palace lawn. They don't weigh much more than half a pound dripping wet.

The most interesting thing about plover is how they decide where to live in Hawaii. Bruner said that decision is made the first time the young birds arrive from Alaska where they hatch. They choose not only the locations but the sizes of their residential lots. "After the choice is made, their territories remain fixed," said Bruner. "Different birds have different-sized territories. We believe this relates to dominance. The more aggressive birds establish larger territories."

On the other hand, not all plover are possessive about owning fee simple land. Some of them seem to prefer to rent and move around. This may be one reason the plover count on the Iolani Palace lawn is not always the same. After counting eleven one week, I counted only seven a week later. Of six plover living at the Capitol the first time, I found only one at home the next. "The tide was probably out and they were having lunch at Keehi Lagoon mud flats," said Ron Walker, state head of forestry and wildlife. "Plover are fascinating and complicated creatures."

They are also not a bird to fool around with. Dr. Ralph Cloward was on the practice tee at Waialae Golf Course when a plover flew into his golf ball. The bird fell dead with a broken neck. As a longtime plover fan, Cloward wanted to have it stuffed and mounted. But the taxidermist refused. He said stuffing a plover requires a special permit under the Migratory Bird Act. It took two years of letter-writing to get the permit. Then Cloward couldn't keep the stuffed bird at home because it must be exhibited only at an educational or scientific institution.

That's why the stuffed plover is sitting in the Punahou School Library.

Sylvester, Hero of Cat–astrophy

Fame, alas, is fleeting. Yet the story of Sylvester is such a heartwarming saga of drama, courage and fortitude in the face of overwhelming odds that it deserves a gentle shove in the direction of immortality.

The story began in May of 1989 when warehousemen at Purina Mills, Inc. in Turlock, California began asking, "I wonder what happened to Sylvester?" About two weeks later, the warehousemen discovered that Sylvester was in Honolulu after giving birth to four kittens in a container of cat food while sailing to Hawaii. Thus a California cat became an overnight celebrity in the 50th State, the darling of cat lovers everywhere and a prime candidate as one of the world's little known important people. How many mothers have started their families while surviving for two weeks in a hot, stuffy cargo container without water, especially mothers who are supposed to be fathers?

Purina's customer service manager, Dick Rossow, said Sylvester was a little black kitten with white whiskers when he...ahhh, she, became the company mascot. "He was very young when we adopted him about a year ago," said Rossow at the time of the great event. "He had the run of a very large warehouse and five loaders took care of him. One of them

took him home and bought him a red collar but Sylvester likes his freedom. He came back to the warehouse. In the five years I've been here, he's the only company pet we've ever had."

What the warehousemen didn't know was that their independent little tomcat was sailing under false colors. Sylvester conducted a secret romance and became pregnant. As the time approached, Sylvester sneaked into a cargo container to nest and have kittens. This particular cargo container proved to be a bad choice. It was loaded with cat food ready for shipment to Hawaii, 2,100 nautical miles to the southwest. The warehousemen slammed the door shut and there was Sylvester locked inside.

So began Sylvester's incredible journey. She rode on a truck from Turlock about 75 miles to the dock in Oakland. How long she waited on the dock nobody knows. Then she was loaded on a Matson Navigation Company container ship and spent five days at sea. The temperature inside a cargo hold with the hatches covered under a tropical sun become very high. Inside a cargo container they become even higher. Here it was, in a little space among packages of cat food, that Sylvester gave birth to four kittens.

Meanwhile, she tore open a package of cat food that showed excellent taste because it was one Purina's best products, Pro Plan. In the heat and darkness, she cared for her little family. The ship sailed into Honolulu Harbor, her captain and crew unaware of the drama being enacted under the deck. In due time, a huge gantry crane lifted the container from the ship's hold and stacked it with hundreds of other huge containers in the enormous container yard. There Sylvester waited again until a truck loaded the container and drove to the warehouse of Fred L. Waldron, Ltd., Honolulu distributor of Purina products.

Bill Thayer, operations manager for Waldron, said Sylvester was discovered when workers opened the container in search of Rodent Lab Chow which is fed to laboratory cats at the

University of Hawaii. Now the drama heightened for animals must not arrive in Hawaii in such informal fashion. To protect the human population against rabies, which is unknown in the Islands, all animals check into the Quarantine Station for a four-months stay. Sylvester's arrival was not only heroic, it was illegal.

"The warehouseman heard meowing in the container so he immediately closed it and we called the Animal Quarantine Station," Thayer said. "Lynn Sakugawa from the station came out and picked up the cat. She was taking it to the quarantine station when we heard the kittens meowing. Two of them were still alive. Lynn had to come back for them." And so Sylvester and her two surviving kittens – starving, dehydrated, half dead – went into the clink.

The keepers at the quarantine station were not required to give Sylvester special treatment. But they immediately saw that she needed attention not available in quarantine. And so Gary Moniz, chief of the operation, bent the rules a little. He recommended that the cat family be hospitalized at the Leeward Pet Clinic near Pearl City.

Now the plot thickens for Gary Moniz is not the only person in Honolulu with a soft heart for cats. It turned out that the cat food distributor's little daughters keep a Siamese called Sasha Jello Cream. Bill Thayer, the cat food distributor, promptly offered to underwrite Sylvester's hospital bills. Then he called the newspaper.

Sylvester's story appeared on the front page of *The Advertiser* the next day with a full report of a visit to the hospital. Veterinarian Edward Gulliver said Sylvester ate two plates of cat food on arrival and drank water like crazy. She was skinny but showed an excellent chance to survive. "With the remaining kittens, it's about fifty-fifty," he said. "Their dehydration rate was about eight percent. At 10 percent they would be comatose and at 12 percent they would be dead. So, you see, it is serious. We will have to tube feed them. They don't have a very strong sucking response, and the mother has a scant amount of milk after going so long without water."

Concern for the welfare of Sylvester and her kittens flooded the newspaper. When the kittens showed signs of revival as Sylvester's milk came back, there were offers for adoption. Thayer said expense was no object. The cat family would stay in the hospital until they were ready to go home. Technically, they were still in quarantine but they lived in plush quarters any fat cat would envy. The kittens became plump and frisky. Sylvester became fat and complacent, letting them romp all over her.

Since quarantine officials ruled that the cat family must return home, Continental Airlines offered three free tickets in the cargo hold of an airliner. Concern mounted that Sylvester's kittens would catch cold at 30,000 feet and a number of travelers insisted on taking the cats home on their laps. In fact, Thayer entertained this idea. But officials at Continental Airlines assured everybody that Sylvester would make the Pacific crossing in luxurious, temperature-and-pressure controlled comfort with plenty of fresh water to drink and the best cat food money can buy.

So it was that Sylvester and her family traveled in a private, fatclass compartment with two other cats and a cocker spaniel from Sydney, Australia. On the night before their departure, Thayer's two daughters – Malia, age 3, and Maisa, age 2 – made cat leis on the kitchen floor with Sasha Jello Cream posing for the lei fittings. When placed in their compartment, Sylvester and her kittens were comfortably settled in a stylish, jet age kennel.

They were greeted in San Francisco, it was reported, by a high-level cat food official, three TV stations and two newspapers. "The kittens are being adopted by Ron Henworth, who works at the mill in Turlock," said Thayer. "An employee named Debbie Elkins is taking Sylvester. I think she plans to have her spayed immediately."

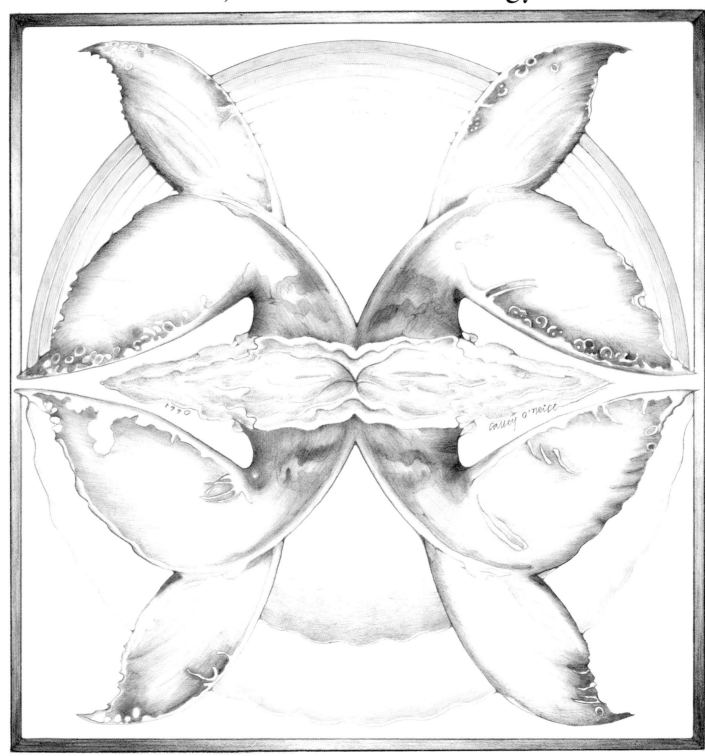

Science In The Back Yard

It is true that Hawaii does not have the reputation of being a world leader in science and technology but this does not mean that we have no interest in understanding how our world is put together. Even common, garden variety citizens make fundamental discoveries in the fields of zoology and botany. Take the scientific drama which unfolded when Victoria Sebetich of Haleiwa was attacked by monarch butterflies. Actually, the butterflies did not attack Victoria. They attacked her crown flowers.

Victoria, who is part Hawaiian, inherited a crown flower business from her mother. The three long rows of crown flower trees in her yard daily produce delicate blossoms which Victoria sells to lei makers who string flowers into garlands for people to wear in the spirit of aloha. What more idyllic livelihood could there be than to loll in the balmy sunshine of Haleiwa while one's crown flower trees cover themselves with blossoms 365 days a year?

It is especially idyllic in winter when ginger is out of season, plumeria trees turn balky, *pikake* gets scarce, *puakenikeni* slows down and *pakalana* is dormant. This is when lei makers pay top prices for Victoria's hardy and ornamental crown flowers. Ahhhh, here's the irony of it. Winter is also the time when the sex-crazed monarch butterfly strikes. It flits around with deceptive grace and beauty, all the while hatching a diabolical plot to destroy Victoria's crown flowers.

In an exclusive interview, Victoria described her battle with butterflies, demonstrating her grasp of the scientific principles involved. "Crown flowers are milk weeds which caterpillars love," she explained. "Caterpillars grow from eggs laid by butterflies. They hide over there, in the mango trees, at night. In the wintertime they come out during the day. If they see a female, they both fall to the ground and mate. Afterward, the female travels from crown flower leaf to crown flower leaf laying eggs. They mate constantly, as many times as they can every day. The female lays eggs all the time. It goes on all winter.

"Each egg becomes a caterpillar that lives about two weeks and does nothing but eat. First it eats the crown flower leaves, then the buds, then the little stems that hold up the buds, then the bark of the trees. There's no medicine that does any good. My father tried to kill the worms with Sprectracide but the leaves fell off the tree. The caterpillars keep eating until the trees are nothing but sticks. In Waianae, I saw a tree with more worms than leaves. The trees over here are bald-headed already."

Here, indeed, is a scientific dilemma of major proportions. To make matters worse, each caterpillar eventually crawls off to a nearby fence or the rafters under the garage to hang upside down and turn itself into a cocoon which soon becomes another sex-mad butterfly. Yet the lei sellers on Maunakea Street can testify that Victoria's trees are among the few that produce flowers during the winter. This is because Victoria has not only undertaken research into the mating habits of monarch butterflies but into the psychology of the adolescent humans. She has discovered the "payoff."

"I have a lot of nephews," she said. "I pay them one cent for every caterpillar they pick, five cents for each butterfly and five cents for each cocoon. My nephews range in age from five years old to seventeen. One nephew yesterday picked 300 caterpillars and $2 worth of butterflies. They can pick 500 butterflies a week, about 2,000 caterpillars and 200 cocoons. It's a good thing there are a lot of kids around here because there's no other way. I paid a nephew six dollars this morning."

The Sexy Side of Serious Science

It would appear, then, that there is a sexy side to science in paradise that may not be so evident in, say, North Dakota or Massachusetts. Unreported scientific research in the 50th State seems to bear this out although few observers other than myself have remarked upon this tropical tendency. Yet it pops up in otherwise unrelated research. This leads me to believe that either professional scientists don't appreciate sex as much as other people or they are too polite to bring up the subject in polite conversation.

For example, I once went to follow up a rumor about the propagation of sea horses at the Waikiki Aquarium, a reputable scientific institution, and ended up with a story about sex-crazed mahimahi. The saga of the sex life of these undersea creatures upon which I stumbled boggles the mind. Here's what happened:

A weekend diver named Jay Huber was swimming off Kailua when he came nose-to-nose with a male sea horse which he captured in his net and brought to the aquarium. Guess what happened? A few days later a whole lot of little sea horses came popping out of their father's abdomen. Yet the aquarium director casually explained that this is not a medical miracle but simply normal procedure; papa sea horses always have the babies. It is the mother who plants the eggs in his pouch. The proud father went on public display in a fish tank out in front while his children played tug-of-war with their tails back in the nursery awaiting their show business debut.

It turned out that the real miracle in this case was not the papa sea horse having babies but an experiment going on behind the show cases. A pioneering scientist named Syd Kraul had learned to develop baby food for infant fish who cannot manage worms and other adult dietary entrees. Kraul explained that baby fish need food in very small bite sizes,

almost too small to see. As they grow older, they can take bigger bites. In the ocean, infant fish can find food in any size they wish. But in aquariums, it's a different matter. So Kraul's propagation of sea horses weaned from microscopic copeods and brine shrimp from teeny-weeny rotifers means that he can produce the food necessary to keep captive baby fish alive. Kraul, then, may be called the undersea Gerber of Hawaii.

It was during this discussion about raising captive fish that I stumbled upon sex-crazed *mahimahi* or dolphin. Kraul found in his work that male mahimahi in captivity become sex maniacs. "The common belief is that mahimahi in the ocean breed in the full moon," he explained. "But in the aquarium, females spawn every other day and the male does it EVERY day. There's a theory about why mahimahi keep dying in aquariums. Actually nobody knows. The theory is that they are having too much sex. We're trying to prove this is not true. So far our male mahimahi is all right after doing it every day for two months. We now believe that the mahimahi die from pollution caused by sperm in the tank water, not from too much sex. By keeping the water clean, we hope to also keep the male mahimahi alive."

Apparently it is not easy. Kraul said a male becomes so crazed by sex that he jumps twenty feet out of the water from sheer enthusiasm during the act. "He crashes into the wall of the fish tank, suffers a fatal concussion and we find him dead the next morning," said Kraul. "We've solved that by designing a fish tank that doesn't give him a chance to jump so far."

This is not an isolated instance of sex in serious science in Hawaii. A colleague in the city room, Jim Borg, *Advertiser* science writer, came upon another instance that may have even greater significance for it edges into the theory of evolution. Borg wrote in 1987, "The long-held notion of the survival of the fittest – the mainstay of Darwin's theory of evolution – is under siege from discoveries about a versatile Hawaiian fruit fly. It appears that female flies, which have the final say in mating, don't necessarily go for the guy who is the strongest, most handsome or the best provider. They fall for the fellow who sings the best love song."

Borg then went on to explain that scientists as far apart as Hawaii and Finland have been recording signals produced by male fruit flies that have flabbergasted everyone in the scientific world. Two types of signals were unknown before because they are produced by the vibration abdominal muscles. These signals appear to be used in fruit fly courtship. "The muscle tones, along with wing vibrations, aphrodisiac perfume, are part of an intricate mating ritual that suggests that sex appeal may be more important than environmental factors in determining what genetic traits are passed on," wrote Borg. He was quoting Kenneth Kaneshiro, director of the Hawaiian Evolutionary Biology Project, who worked with Roy Hoy of Cornell University and Anneli Hoikkaala of the University of Oulu in Finland.

"Some females are incredibly picky about mating," wrote Borg. "The courtship 'dance' can last for more than an hour without success. Other females are less discriminating. Kaneshiro argues that choosiness is an advantage for populations that are well established, since it allows the female to be sure that she is mating with a fly of her own species and not a close...cousin. In newly established populations...choosiness is a disadvantage since talented suitors are at a premium." 'Loose' females who have a lot of little fruit flies, therefore, allow the small population to grow and become established. However, research seems to indicate that once the population becomes firmly established the female becomes more picky and her choice of a suitor more important in determining which genes will be passed on.

Can You See Mauna Kea?

Let us now turn from Hawaiian zoology to a mystery in the field of Island meteorology. It is a debate that began years ago and has been waged since with unflagging enthusiasm by amateur scientists who cannot agree whether anybody has ever seen the island of Hawaii from the island of Oahu. You can do your own research the next time you stop at Diamond Head lookout or at the Blow Hole. Cast your eyes on the southern horizon and see what there is to see. Just don't call me with your results. I've resigned as coordinator of CYSMKFDHRP (Can You See Mauna Kea From Diamond Head Research Project).

However, I am willing to pass along minutes of past meetings. It all began one exceptionally clear morning in December 1980. While walking the beach in Kailua, Oahu, a Navy officer thought he saw the peak of Mauna Kea on the Big Island. He ran home and grabbed his sextant. Sure enough, his calculations worked out. The peak of Mauna Kea was right where it was supposed to be on the horizon.

His neighbor telephoned me. Skeptical, I decided to check before publishing this unexpected breakthrough. First, I called James McFeely who was traffic controller for Honolulu harbor. The traffic controller raises and lowers the balls on top of Aloha Tower which signal ships to enter and leave the harbor. "Can you see Mauna Kea from the Aloha Tower on a clear day?" I asked.

"Hell, you can't see Diamond head from here, much less Mauna Kea," he answered scientifically.

"What if the high rises weren't in the way?"

"That's got to be over 200 miles. I don't think you can see that far. And if you could, it ain't never THAT clear. The only thing I can think of is somebody on top of a 30-story condo in Whacky-key with powerful binocs might do it."

The next call went to Captain Donald Gately, harbor master for Honolulu. "I doubt if you can see Mauna Kea from Oahu," he said. "It's because of the curvature of the earth. If you watch a ship going over the horizon, it drops out of sight. If it's 20 feet high, it disappears faster than if it's 100 feet high. I'm sure you can't see a 13,796-foot mountain from 150 miles away. What they're probably seeing is cloud structure."

Armed with this expertise, I called Captain Frank Kapele, then port captain for Dillingham Tug & Barge, a veteran of countless voyages inter-island and to the West Coast. "No, I've never seen Mauna Kea from Oahu but I've talked to people who say they have," he told me. "What they might have seen is Haleakala on Maui. If it had snow on it, it was probably Mauna Kea because the snow on Haleakala usually melts a few hours after the sun comes up. It would have to be an exceptionally clear day. If you're lucky, you get maybe one or two days like that a year. Maybe you could see it, though. There's a formula for how far you can see but I haven't figured it out."

Gately suggested I get in touch with Captain Bob "Two Stack" McKenzie, longtime love boat skipper and chief of maritime operations for Matson Navigation Company in Hawaii at the time. "I've never seen Mauna Kea from Oahu," he said. "I have seen Maui and Lanai. Tell you what, let me get out my Bowditch and call you back."

That's what he did. Now get ready to take notes because here' where we get down to the nitty-gritty. "All right," said McKenzie, "We took the longitude at Diamond Head and the height of Mauna Kea figured at 13,368 feet. It figures out that you can see that height on an absolutely clear day for 137 miles. By coincidence, Mauna Kea is 137 miles from Diamond Head. So it would be right on the horizon. You can't see it."

Good! The subject was settled. Now I could go on to more important matters like getting a haircut. But just as I was about to hang up the phone, McKenzie added, "How-ever, there's something called refraction. It's when you pass through cold weather, a mountain will rise right out of the sea. I've seen Santa Rosa light from 100 miles when it's good for only 28. I've seen the Farallon Islands stand high on the horizon and sink as you approach. I've seen as many as three lights from the Farallon lighthouse, one over the other. So you might be able to see Mauna Kea from Oahu under those conditions. You don't usually have refractions in this climate but maybe it's cold on the mountain."

Hmmmmmmm. That complicated matters somewhat. Oh well, nobody would pay attention anyway. I was about to hang up again when McKenzie added, "On the other hand, draw a straight line between Diamond Head and Mauna Kea with a ruler and you'll see that Lanai gets in the way. Draw a line from Kailua Beach to Mauna Kea and both Molokai and Lanai get in the way. What people are seeing is Lanai. They think it's Mauna Kea."

Letters and telephone calls began coming in the day after this report appeared. First, amateur photographer Tim Haehnlen submitted a photograph taken on an incredibly clear day from Hawaii Kai which proved absolutely that you can't see the Big Island from Oahu. Clearly etched on the skyline were Molokai, Maui and Lanai, but no Hawaii.

Then a reliable eye witness, real estate agent Albert Sur, came forward to swear that he had seen Mauna Kea from Kahuku in the 1940s. "It was during World War II," he said. "I was in charge of a six-man squad guarding the Kahuku airstrip. We had a mortar position on a hill at about 1,000 feet elevation. One cold, clear morning I saw Mauna Kea. It had snow on it and it was just to the left of Lanai. Haleakala was to the left of Mauna Kea. I know it was Mauna Kea because I'm from the Big Island and I know the outline of that mountain."

Our next witness is Thurston Twigg-Smith who has worked his way up from office boy to president of *The Honolulu*

Advertiser. He swears that he's seen Mauna Kea from Oahu not once but twice: "Both times were in the late '40s when I was in the circulation department and, hence, up regularly in the predawn hours. On the first occasion, a fantastically clear morning, I whisked up to the level of the tunnel entrance on Diamond Head and there was everything: two levels of Molokai, Maui, Lanai, Kahoolawe AND a distant and very clear additional island. I was so sure it was the Big Island that I told Joe Ogle, then an artillery major and adviser to my National Guard artillery battalion. He scoffed. However, since he lived at Ruger he agreed to come the next time with a plane table, sighting device, map, etc. The next time I saw it he came and when we laid the aiming device on the plane table, it pointed directly toward the Big Island."

The weirdest story of all came from Miles Kinley, U.S. Army retired, who attended a consciousness arousing seminar on top of Koko Head at dawn on August 13, 1978. Now see if you believe what Kinley said he saw: "We were sitting there when light began to appear. That was before the sun came up. Off in the distance, you could see all the islands. I could see Hawaii. Not just the mountain tops but the whole island. It looked like a stage setting, as if the Big Island was only a few miles away. The ocean was absolutely flat calm. As the sun began to peep over the horizon, the islands began to move away. It wasn't all of a sudden but gradually. The islands literally moved away from us. By the time the sun came over the horizon, the only island we could see was Molokai."

Most people are lucky if they can make out Rabbit Island 500 yards off the Makapuu Lookout. But don't give up. Keep your eyes peeled on the horizon. There's no telling what you might see.

Baby, It's Cold Inside

The weather in Hawaii is not normally a topic of much scientific interest because perfection does not lend itself to study. How many experiments do you have to make to find out that the year around average temperature on Waikiki Beach is 75 degrees?

There was a slight stirring of interest a few years ago when the National Weather Service announced that Honolulu is the fourth windiest city in the U.S. behind Mt. Washington, New Hampshire; Boston, Massachusetts; and Buffalo, New York. Chicago, the Windy City, ranked only 11th. But even the wind in Hawaii has a benevolent quality. That's what keeps the tropical temperature and humidity under control.

Had modern technology been content to let the Northeast trade wind continue to regulate our climate, everything would be fine. But, no, somebody had to tinker with nature and that is why the most unpredictable weather in the 50th state is not found outside under the palm trees but INSIDE under air conditioning ducts. When something goes wrong with the air conditioner, you could be anywhere from deep in the Amazon to Point Barrow, Alaska.

That's what happened on a balmy summer day when I came to work in my walking shorts. The city room was like a deep freeze. Gerry Keir, now editor, sat huddled behind his computer terminal shivering in a sweater. My knees turned blue. This is what prompted me to do some basic research on indoor weather in Hawaii. I called a thermometer distributor.

"It is so cold in my office I'm about to come down with pneumonia," I explained. "What I want to do is take the temperature and compare it with other offices downtown. Do you have a thermometer that gives instant readings?"

The lady on the other end said, "We don't have anything like that but I can tell you it's cold in here. I have to bring a sweater to work. Why don't you try Berkley Engineering in Kalihi?"

An hour later, Peter Hansen, Berkley's president, had equipped me with a digital thermometer that is so sensitive it will jump five degrees when placed near the hot air vent of a politician. This gadget enabled me to make a number of landmark discoveries about our town. To wit: The coldest place in Honolulu is the Amfac board room, 67 degrees, on the 17th floor of the Amfac Tower. There's more. Temperatures in air conditioned office buildings vary more than 10 degrees, from Amfac's 67 to 77.3 on the 18th floor of Bank Corp. Building at Bishop and King Streets.

Additional research indicated that the key factor here may be the metabolism of the chairman and chief executive officer of the company that owns the building. Henry Walker, chairman of Amfac, and Robert Reed, chairman/president/chief executive officer of Pacific Resources Inc., sat on top of two of the coldest buildings in town. Reed's office measured a frigid 69 and Walker's 70.8. A blast of cold air blew out of Walker's office like a gale off Cape Horn. By comparison, Bank of Hawaii chairman and CEO Frank Manaut basked in a balmy 75 degrees and the highest indoor temperatures downtown were in the Bank of Hawaii Building.

At Amfac Tower it was so cold that Sandy Ebesu on the 17th floor wore a sweater and kept a heater under her desk. The city's coldest receptionist was Nanette Hookano on the sixth floor of the HGEA building at Queen and Mililani Streets. It was 71.2 degrees on top of her desk and 70.8 on the floor where she kept her heater. Another refrigerator was the Pacific Tower at King and Alakea Streets. Attorney Bryan Y. Y. Ho sat right under an air conditioning vent on the 29th floor. The temperature at his desk was 68 degrees.

But the temperatures were not consistent from floor to floor, or even from office to office on the same floor, in any building I measured. For some reason, the coldest place on the 18th floor of the Bank Corp. Building was the men's john. In the Pacific Tower, the warmest place was the women's john. That's where chicken skin office workers went to warm their hands under the hot water tap.

"The temperature indoors is a lot more complicated than outside," said Sharon Simpson, a legal assistant in the Pacific Tower. "It used to get so hot in here I had to buy a fan. I finally got somebody to fix the air conditioning. Now it's too cold but I'm afraid to say anything. You don't know what could happen next."

"You can't figure it out," said Evelyn, in charge of special events in the Bank Corp. Building. "When we close one vent, the cold air comes out stronger someplace else. I don't know why but the ninth floor is cooler than all the rest in our building."

How To Read The Tail of a Whale

Pacific whales did not begin as subjects of scientific research in Hawaii but as an economic resource and symbols of adventure. Stories of whaling voyages – frail humans pitted against behemoths of the deep – were grist for adventure writers. But now it is the whale that we feel sorry for. Like the buffalo, whales have been hunted so relentlessly that they are far more a curiosity than a threat. Boatloads of whale watchers with binoculars and cameras depart daily from the Lahaina Harbor on Maui to stalk families of humpbacks at a respectful distance during the whaling season.

It is to this exotic pastime, whale watching, that science has added a whole new dimension. For the first time since Captain Ahab identified Moby Dick out of thousands of whales that roam the vast Pacific, you can do the same. All you need is a good look at the tail of your whale as he or she dives, and a copy of *Humpback Whales of the Central & Eastern North Pacific* to see which whale it is. This University of Hawaii Sea Grant Program publication shows photos of the tails of more than 650 whales that swim down from Alaska to winter in Hawaii.

You will notice as you turn the pages of this unusual book that some of the whales' tails in the photos – they are also called flukes – have chunks bitten out of them. Some tails seem to be bigger than others, like ears in humans. The greatest difference in the whales' tails is the white markings on their undersides. No two whales have the same markings.

"The tails of humpback whales are much like fingerprints of humans for identification purposes," explained Dr. Louis M. Herman, director of the Kewalo Basin Marine Mammal Laboratory in Honolulu, the only research facility of its kind in the world. He has been researching whales for 20 years.

Not only is each whale's tail distinctive but the white markings do not change from youth to old age, pointed out researcher Joseph R. Mobley, a coauthor of the whales' tail catalogue. "One whale has been tracked for 17 years, and there has been no change in the markings of its tail," he said. "We call this whale Garfunkle."

Think of what this book will do for whale watching. Now teenagers can collect photos of their favorite whales as they would of movie or rock stars. Sports fans can trade whales' tail photos like baseball cards. The Hawaii State Legislature might run a competition to pick the State Whale. Those who are deep into roots can even use the whales' tail photos to study the genealogies of their favorite whales.

You see, Pacific whales tend to spend the summer on feeding grounds off Alaska, then swim south for the winter. Some of them go to California, some to Hawaii. It is believed that relatives tend to stick together. Another coauthor of the book, C. Scott Baker, is tracing the family trees of whales by their tail markings, among other things, on the assumption that whales who share the same summer feeding grounds off Alaska are of the same family.

But when they swim south to Hawaii or California for a winter in the sun, a strange thing happens. The families seem to intermingle, sort of like tourists in Waikiki. It is at this time that romance takes place. Yet, in spite of this indiscriminate mingling, girl whales must prefer nice boy whales from their own families because the family markings seem to be perpetuated. You can easily see that serious whale watchers have only begun to scratch the surface.

There is a lot more to learn about whales and that is why Herman encourages whale watchers to take photos of whales' tails to compare with those in the catalogue or to add to it. On the photo you should write the date it was taken, the time of day, the location and some information about what the whale was doing. Was it alone or with another whale? Was a calf along?

Herman advised one word of caution. "It can be very noisy for whales under water," he said. The outboard motor on your boat sounds like a very angry bee to a whale nearly a mile away. Herman said he's seen whales react to the approach of large passenger ships at a distance of fifteen miles. So stay at least the length of a football field away from the whales and use a telephoto lens for getting close. Remember to keep the sun at your back so it will shine on the whale's tail and not on your face. And be patient.

"Photographing a whale's tail is like taking pictures of your baby," said Mobley. "You have to wait and wait until it dives and then shoot at just the right moment."

Sports in Hawaii

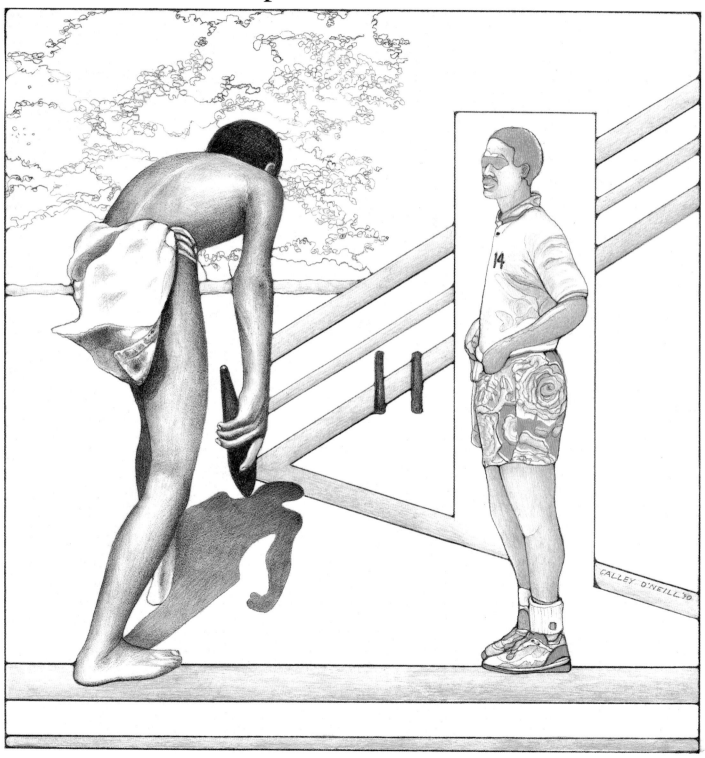

Baseball, The Art of Delayed Gratification

By all accounts, the old Hawaiians were tremendous athletes. Chiefs competed fiercely in surfing matches and spear throwing exercises. Kamehameha the Great was a professional in both. Tales have come down about legendary runners, and canoemen who were so strong they could get from Waianae to Waikiki with one stroke of the paddle. An old Maui warrior, tattooed black on one side, Kahekili by name, was a noted jumper off of cliffs. Kahekili's Leap on the leeward side of Lanai was his favorite place to have a little fun. Other ancient jocks, the iron pumpers of their day, could lift stones the size of Volkswagens.

After the missionaries arrived, local folks lost in muscle tone what they gained in Bible verses because the missionaries came down hard on idle amusements. They promoted prayer, instead, which was good for the soul but didn't do much to develop the biceps. The traditional Hawaiian sports fell into disfavor, especially surfing, an activity practiced in the near nude. So you can see that athletes in Hawaii had obstacles to overcome before they got to the World Series.

This may be one reason why local college teams seldom make the national rankings, or win national championships nor are often chosen to play in bowl games after the season is over. There are occasional moments of sporting glory in paradise like when the University of Hawaii football team beat powerhouse Nebraska on the road in the 1950s and little Chaminade College out in Kaimuki upset the University of Virginia, ranked number one in basketball, in the 1970s. But mostly sports fans practice the art of delayed gratification.

It is fitting, therefore, that we begin our essay about sports in Hawaii with a tribute to this specialized aspect of the game. After all, somebody has to lose. You can't always have what you want. Delayed gratification is good for the moral fiber of the nation. Our ancestors knew this because everything was delayed before reaching Hawaii including results of the two most popular sports in paradise, baseball and politics. Honolulu was 2,100 nautical miles from the nearest telegraph. News had to come by ship.

It was in November 1888 that sports fans in Hawaii turned delayed gratification into a fine art. That was the year *The Advertiser* announced that America's top professional baseball players had agreed to play an exhibition game during a stopover enroute to Australia and other capitols of the world. The tour was sponsored by millionaire A. G. Spalding, owner of the Chicago club and of a sporting goods firm, and would introduce professional baseball to the palm trees of Hawaii, the pyramids of Egypt and the Coliseum of Rome.

Understand, Hawaii's athletes had been playing the game since 1867 but not in a professional manner. The King's Band squared off against the Honolulu Mechanics. The Kahului Dudes batted against the Spreckelsville Plantation Nine. The *U.S.S. Pensacola*, anchored in Honolulu Harbor, got together a team to play the hot shot local Oceanics, and so forth. Now Honolulu baseball fans would finally get to see future Hall of Famers like star Chicago outfielder King Kelly, catcher Cap Anson with a batting average of .344, and New York shortstop John Montgomery Ward, not to be confused with the mail order business.

The excitement in baseball circles was exceeded only by the euphoria exhibited by fans of Hawaii's other favorite sport, politics, because the United States was having a presidential election that fall and the campaign was in full cry. As a monarchy, Hawaii voters didn't vote for presidents but that didn't stop local sports fans from enjoying the action wherever it might be.

Blue jackets from the *U.S.S. Brooklyn* in Honolulu Harbor came out strong for Democrat Grover Cleveland, not to be confused with National League pitcher Grover Cleveland Alexander. Sailors on board the *U.S.S. Alert* stood firmly for Republican Benjamin Harrison, not to be confused with "Moon" Harris of the Boston Red Sox. On shore, American citizens held a political rally in a vacant store at Fort and Hotel Streets, then organized a mock election in which leading citizens of Honolulu voted.

On the baseball front, fans of the sport including King David Kalakaua and the Chamber of Commerce, went into action to provide a memorable greeting for the first professional baseball stars to visit Hawaii. They held tryouts to form a local All Star team to play the professionals. The King promised an audience with the baseball stars and the Chamber of Commerce organized a big luau. All of these exciting events would take place between the time the steamer *Alameda* arrived from San Francisco in the morning and departed for Sydney, Australia in the evening.

With plans laid, delayed gratification set in. The U.S. presidential election came and went. Nobody in the country knew for sure who got elected because it took time to count all the votes and send in the results. A week passed, two weeks before accurate predictions could be made. It would take another week for the news to reach Hawaii by ship.

Familiar with this problem, political sports fans in Hawaii arranged for signals to be relayed from the ship by friends returning from San Francisco on board the *Alameda* when the steamer arrived off Waikiki. A U.S. flag flying from the foremast meant that McKinley had won, a Hawaiian flag meant that Harrison had won, and so forth. Some half a dozen separate sets of signals were prepared by various groups, each intent on getting the news first.

Baseball enthusiasts were just as busy. They lined up the Royal Hawaiian Band to go off port on a tug boat and tootle

Aloha Oe to the arriving athletes. Leading citizens signed up to go along, willing to get seasick for the privilege of shaking hands personally with a baseball star.

Alas, the ship was delayed. It came in a day late. Also, so many flags fluttered and signals flashed from off Waikiki that nobody could figure out who got elected president until the ship arrived at the dock, which took all the fun out of it. Also, the *Alameda* arrived on Sunday. In Honolulu, hardly anything was permitted on the Sabbath except shallow breathing. Chinese got hauled in for playing checkers. Kite flying was kapu. To play baseball would be unthinkable. So the world's greatest baseball stars met the King and learned to eat poi. But they did not play a single inning of the great national sport. Never has our Hawaii felt so deeply the joy of delayed gratification.

This probably explains the fierce loyalty exhibited by local sports fans for the University of Hawaii Rainbow baseball team, coached by a deadpan Japanese-American, Les Murakami. The baseball Rainbows are one of the few local teams that consistently make the national rankings.

Peacocks of Volleyball

Hawaii has become a powerhouse in one other college sport besides baseball. That sport is volleyball, an activity that was practiced for years on beach outings and during picnics in the park between the chicken and the beer. In recent years, however, volleyball has shed its back yard image because it's faster than basketball, as scientific as baseball and is played all over the world. It's an Olympic sport. When the first Russians arrived in Hawaii on a science ship, the first thing they wanted to do was play volleyball.

The Rainbow Wahines (women) volleyball team at the

University of Hawaii broke into the big time about ten years ago and has won several national championships since. Now the Rainbow Men have climbed into the national rankings for the ferocity of their play and into the headlines because of the fancy pants they wear. No other team in the country can match the Rainbow Men for razzle dazzle between the waist and the knees. "I've gotten calls and letters from all over the country asking us where we get our shorts," said Alan Rosehill, team coach. "There was a fellow in New York wanted to know where he can buy some."

The Rainbow Men brought high fashion to collegiate volleyball in 1988. They were back for the 1989 season with psychedelic uniforms that were even more, ...ahhhhhhh... stunning. In their home opener, they won two games against Loyola University in shorts done in panels of eye-catching green and white. For the third game, they clobbered their opponents while wearing wavy tiger stripes. The Loyola team, dressed in traditional solid red, looked like bankers playing the Waikiki Beach All Stars.

Rosehill said his team, ranked first in the nation at the time, keeps about six different pairs of shorts in the closet, all in the latest shades of orange, blue, green and yellow, ready to spring on unsuspecting opponents. After all, the team is nicknamed the "Rainbows." This wardrobe is a far cry from the previous four years of the beginning volleyball program when the players wore their own shorts to practice and had to hustle to the laundromat after every game on the road because the university issued only two uniforms per player.

The Rainbow Men are now known as the best-dressed volleyball team in the nation and may become trend setters for the entire sports uniform industry. At the University of California in Los Angeles, the women's volleyball teams has adopted the same fast-forward look. The UCLA football team liked it so well the players asked for jackets in that style to wear to the Cotton Bowl.

Rosehill said the man responsible for the Rainbow image is Dave Rochlen, president of a locally based sportswear company called Surf Line Hawaii Ltd., the originator of JAMS. The first set of uniforms donated to the Rainbow Men by Rochlen were in colors that can be charitably described as non-traditional. The next set was even more so. One style of shorts had a wide elastic waistband like prize fighters wear in the ring. Except these shorts were decorated with enormous roses in lavender and pink. Then there was a style called Neon Check with a design of squares on colors that would light the Wilson Tunnel.

"I've put the team under a lot of pressure having them wear these uniforms," admitted Rosehill. "They have to make a stronger statement (play better) when they're in them. But I feel it's our responsibility to take that stance. We could be like anybody else. Nobody else in the country wears uniforms like we do.

To learn more about where collegiate sports uniforms are going, I drove out to Surf Line for a chat with Rochlen. In my Reyn's reverse-pattern, button-down aloha shirt I felt like an undertaker at a surfing meet. Rochlen said most teams wear solid colors because that's what the major surfing companies put out. "The Rainbows are way ahead in collegiate uniqueness," he assured me. "They're wearing what Olympic bikers and skaters and skiers wear. It's the fast-forward look, not the dumb stuff."

He said he has great plans for future Rainbow uniforms: "High-tech fabrics, stuff that is like paper, has a good drape and takes color magnificently." Rochlen said he has considered donating bikinis instead of regular shorts. But that might be too far out even for the Rainbows. "The way the players slam down on the floor and skid on the wood, bikini shorts may not be practical," he admitted. "Not unless they wear hip pads."

Dancing on the Waves

If Hawaii is America's Pacific outpost of baseball and a pioneer breeding ground for volleyball, the Islands are the undisputed world capitol of surfing. Other Pacific islanders ride the waves but Hawaiians were the best long before Europeans discovered the sport. That is because the conformation of the coastline in Hawaii produces better surf for riding than shorelines on other islands and atolls. The sport was so important in old Hawaii that there were surfing *heiaus* or temples.

And it is from Hawaii that the sport spread around the world. A Waikiki water rat named George Freeth, nicknamed the "Brown Mercury" by writer Jack London, taught Californians to surf at Redondo Beach in 1907. The legendary Duke Kahanamoku introduced surfing in 1912 to Australia. But it was not until 1986 that the land of Confucius and Mao Tse Tung first took lessons on a surfboard. An American safari sponsored by *Surfer* magazine took the trip at the invitation of the Chinese government which was interested in making China more competitive in Western sports. The champion U.S. professional surfers were Matt George and Willy Morris of California, and Jon Damm and Rell Sunn-Shaner of Hawaii. Honolulu ace surf photographer Warren Bolster went along to record the historic event.

Sunn-Shaner, a perceptive and hang-loose lady who worked as a lifeguard at Makaha Beach when not on the world professional surfing circuit, said the Chinese government bussed in about fifty teenage students for five days to learn the new sport. She said both males and females were excellent swimmers and were enthusiastic about surfing. Adult members of the Chinese press, sent to cover the action, also tried to catch waves. It took a while before they accepted the informality of it all.

"They are geared to greatness," Sunn-Shaner said. "They don't like to fail. But they kept falling off their boards. One of them came in and said, 'How can failing be so much fun?' One thing they picked up on is the freedom of surfing. Once you step into the ocean, you're on your own. One of the journalists came out of the water and said, 'I never felt so free in my life.' Surfing is just so new, so foreign, so alien to them. We were the first surfers in China. We took our surfboards to the Great Wall and played Frisbee in the square at Beijing. You know, they don't do anything foolish like that. Their faces don't have laugh lines."

Damm, who lives in Kailua, said, "The word for surfing in Chinese means 'dancing on the waves.' They don't have an image of surfers as kids who don't work and take drugs. They look at it more as an arty, gymnastic type of sport, like dancing. The people there seem to latch onto the subtleties and finesse of surfing more than people in middle America."

He said the surfing classes took place at Hainan Island off the south China coast. They found a shore break of three to five feet similar to waves in Florida but not "world class." In spite of the enthusiasm of the students and the journalists, Damm said he cannot picture the Chinese adopting a spontaneous, free-and-easy surfing lifestyle.

"I can't see it becoming a national sport," he said. "They look at it more like gymnastics. They'll find a good surf spot and build housing there for students who have the ability. They'll take them at an early age and train them every day to surf. This rubs out surfing in China as a sport anybody on the beach can take up. They're too busy making a living and surfboards cost too much. We didn't see anybody using the miles of beaches on the island."

Sunn-Shaner said the surfers found Chinese ways just as

unfamiliar as the Chinese found theirs: "We saw horses with carts in the middle of the road. Everybody rides bicycles. A station wagon is a bicycle with a board in back where four children can ride. The food we ate was great to frightening. At Hainan it was real gnarly. We had ox genitals which we were told at first were cuttlefish. We ate dog, cat, rat, monkey, snake and mynah bird (Damm called it pigeon). Nothing is fat there. The meat is so dry the guys called it chainsaw chicken. The vegetables were cooked in so much oil we made jokes about it being 30 or 40 weight."

Sunn-Shaner said the Chinese thought it "strange to always look for the perfect wave, to think of a sunset as important. They ask, 'Why is it that Americans always romanticize their thoughts?' They were curious about when I started surfing (at age four) and when I became aware of the world. I said I found a glass ball on the beach when I was seven. My father told me it came from Japan. These people can become very good surfers. Look at what happened in Australia. The Chinese can do the same thing. They're all high-tech like rocket scientists. They're very competitive. It won't take them long to become champions."

Pipi Wakayama, Football Hero

While Hawaii is not noted as a powerhouse on the gridiron, there is among us a football celebrity known the length and breadth of the United States among the greatest stars ever produced by the sport. The chances are you have never heard of this paragon. But ask Joe Montana, legendary quarterback of the San Francisco 49ers, or coach Mike Ditka, of the Chicago Bears, and you will get instant recognition. These are among the hundreds of top collegiate football players who have been chosen over the years to compete in the annual Hula Bowl in Honolulu. It is there that they have come under the spell of an undersized, over-aged, glum-faced photographer named Pipi Wakayama.

Earl Campbell, Franco Harris, Frank Gifford, Eric Dickerson, Marcus Allen, Tony Dorsett, O. J. Simpson and Dan Marino all belong to the Pipi Wakayama school of photography because it is his job to immortalize their images singly and in a group with his camera for the Hula Bowl. When Pipi went to the hospital for a back operation in 1988, a get-well letter arrived from the entire New York Jets team. You know why? Because Pipi photographed Joe Walton, the Jets coach, when he went to the Hula Bowl in 1957 for the University of Pittsburgh. And Walton never forgot. Jets wide receiver Al Toon sent his personal player's jersey. The jersey is too big in the chest even for Arnold Schwarzenegger and it hangs down to Pipi's knees but he's proud of it.

A few months later a letter came in the mail from R. C. "Alley Oop" Owen, executive assistant for the San Francisco 49ers. He played in the Hula Bowl in 1967 and Pipi took his photo. It turned out that Alley Oop's daughter wanted to get married by a waterfall in Hawaii. Alley Oop immediately thought of his old friend, Pipi, and wrote to ask him to arrange the following for April 26:

1. A justice of the peace.
2. Wedding location by a convenient waterfall.
3. A photographer.
4. Dinner for eight people.
5. Flower leis for the wedding party.

"Imagine, I never seen him since 1967," Pipi marveled. "Chee, after all these years he trusts me to find him a waterfall. I don't know how he got my phone number. He never could pronounce my name."

One reason the great football stars remember Pipi is because he calls the signals and they MOVE: "Hey, back row has to go left. You in the middle, I can't see da face. SMILE! Where you think you are, in bed?" Doris Obata Kumple, now a resident of Long Island, New York, explained another clue to Pipi's popularity. "When I was living in Honolulu in the 1950s, Pipi brought Paul Horning to one of our New Year's Eve parties," she recalled. "The next day he stopped at our home with three of the Hula Bowl players to eat traditional Japanese food."

Pipi said that was no big deal because, in those days, the Hula Bowl couldn't afford to entertain the players. "When somebody wanted to go shopping, I take 'em," he said. "One year, two players from Notre Dame had to go to church every morning. I took 'em to St. Augustine's in Waikiki. They kneel in there, you know. Every morning I'm in there kneeling. Ohhhhh, my knees sore."

Pipi has filled four huge albums with photos of his clients, the nation's all-time football greats. He has a closet full of sweatshirts and jerseys from every team in the National Football League. At his age, he isn't as spry as before so he closed his studio on King Street and he unlimbers his camera only for the Hula Bowl and the Pro Bowl. But he still maintains a hole-in-the-wall darkroom in Kaimuki to develop the prints. "It's hard to find," he admitted. "You got to go back inside one alley and if you bigger than five feet five you bump your head on the ceiling."

Boola Boola to the Hula Hula

It may come as a surprise to discover that there are football fans who have traveled 5,000 miles from the birthplace of the sport all the way to Hawaii to learn the fine points of the game. Yet it is true. It happened when the Yale Bulldogs arrived in Aloha Land to tangle with the University of Hawaii Rainbows. Naturally, the Bulldogs brought with them their cheerleaders and a herd of Yale alumni.

It is important here to understand that Yale alumni are unlike alumni in, say, Nebraska where they charter fleets of airplanes, wear red T-shirts and caps, and generally overflow whatever stadium on the road in which the Cornhuskers are scheduled. Yale alumni are relatively well behaved by comparison and they travel first class. They tend to be judges and secretaries of state and presidents of the Rockefeller Foundation or the Morgan Trust Company. And they don't wear red T-shirts.

Nevertheless, the lure of Hawaii brought quite a sizable contingent to watch the Bulldogs get beaten again. One attraction was the Hawaii chapter of Yale alumni, a distinguished collection of lawyers, doctors and other people who live on Kahala Avenue. The local chapter arranged all sorts of pleasant social affairs and, most important of all, a pep rally in a tropical amphitheater where the Kodak Hula Show gives performances. The local alumni even got up a pep band to play *Boola Boola*, the Yale classic school song written by a student from Hawaii.

Never having covered a Yale pep rally, I attended this distinguished gathering only to find it unlike any pep rally in my experience. For some reason, the Yale alumni didn't know how to act. They sat under the hot sun like the board of directors for Prudential Life Insurance Company. One of the members of the band gave me a clue as to what was the matter.

"You know, I can't remember ever playing for a pep rally before," said trumpet player Wally English, class of '58. "I played trumpet for four years in the Yale band but only at football games. I don't think we ever had a pep rally."

John Derby on cymbals agreed. "I graduated in 1963 and played all four years in the Yale band. Now that you mention it, I can't remember a pep rally."

Surely somebody at Yale must, in the school's long history, have attended a pep rally so I went into the stands to find him or her. Frank D. O'Reilly, class of '36, is a retired newspaper publisher. "It's been a long time ago but I can't remember going to a pep rally while I was at Yale," he said. "Maybe we thought they weren't sophisticated."

Tom McCance, class of '55, a Yale fund-raiser, said flatly, "There never has been one since at least 1955. That's why this is such a great event for the football team."

I immediately made up my mind that here was a sports story of incredible significance, the first pep rally in the history of Yale. And it was being held in Hawaii. To make sure I had the facts straight, I asked student cheerleaders Sue Virguto, a sophomore, and Laura Sprague, a senior, who came out from New Haven for the game. "We were supposed to have one for the first game this year but it rained," said Sue.

Coach Carm Cozza introduced the seniors on the football team. A lot of them looked more like advertising executives than fullbacks. He said the Yale team included nine players who were valedictorians of their high school classes, 23 who were in the top ten (not 10 percent) of their classes, 36 who were captains of their high school football teams, and 41 who were national honor society students. Cozza said he's coached 2,000 football players at Yale and only five have not graduated. "The only dummies on this team are the coaches," he admitted.

Although inexperienced, the Yale alumni took to the pep rally like, if you will pardon the expression, a bulldog takes to cats. Present in attendance was a real, live bulldog, stand-in for Yale mascot Handsome Dan the 13th. He didn't wake up until the cheerleaders came on. The pickup band tootled *Boola Boola*, composed by Sunny Cunha from Honolulu, and *Bulldog, Bulldog, Bow Wow Wow* by Cole Porter. One of the alumni even waved a banner. It read, "For God, For Country, And For Yale."

Pearls and Golf Balls

Golf arrived in Hawaii in the 1890s when a few pioneers including Walter F. Dillingham, later a major tycoon, knocked some balls around on a rocky slope in Manoa Valley hard by Punahou School. The players carved out the first proper course in Nuuanu Valley in 1906 and established the Oahu Country Club. While most of our residents were too busy hoeing and harvesting sugar cane to find time for putting, the hard core held tournaments every year.

Demands for a municipal golf course started in the 1920s. By the time Hawaii became a state in 1959, golf had become a favorite way to spend the weekend. The Hawaiian Open kicked off in 1965 with barefoot caddies at the Waialae Country Club which had once been pasture land for a dairy. Now every self-respecting destination resort advertises at least one eighteen-hole golf course. Golf courses have become such gold mines that developers swamped the City & County of Honolulu Planning Department with 30 requests for golf course permits before the mayor finally declared a moratorium.

Golfers in Hawaii, therefore, come in all shapes and sizes and speak practically every language under the sun. But none of the breed are more enthusiastic than *wahine* (women) golfers who have developed their own approach to the sport that deserves serious consideration. The day I spent with the ladies at their Waialae Women's Invitational Golf Tournament convinced me that male tournament promoters can learn something from the women.

Scoring, for example.

The females at Waialae have made a revolutionary discovery that helped turn their tournament into the most popular golfing event for women in our Islands. Instead of just picking a winner, they give away as many prizes as possible.

The player with the fewest net strokes received ten long

strands of freshwater pearls and a trophy. The player with the fewest gross number of strokes got eight strands. First place winner in each of five flights got six strands. Second, third, fourth place winners, etc., in each flight got pearls. That's enough pearls to stock a jewelry store.

There were prizes for the longest ball hit off number ten tee and for getting closest to the pin on number 16 green. Had a woman golfer made a hole in one on number eight she would have driven home in a new Toyota to use for a year. There were 50 door prizes for 144 golfers no matter what their score. One out of every three women got a door prize just for showing up. Finally, every woman lucky enough to get into the tournament walked out with a pot of chrysanthemums and a wallet. All this plus a gourmet luncheon and three days of golf at a price of only $52 per golfer.

The woman who performed this economic miracle is Penny Wells, invitational chairwoman. She seems a natural candidate for Secretary of Defense. With her talent for low cost procurement, she could have the country out of debt in six months.

"Men spend a whole lot more money," said Margie Walinski from the Honolulu International Country Club over by Salt Lake. "They think nothing of paying $400 to get into a tournament. They have more betting going, too. Where women will bet a quarter on putts, men bet $100."

The biggest difference between the way men and women play golf seems to be in their attitude toward winning. I took a little survey about what the ladies look for in a golf tournament. "What I like about playing in this tournament is meeting the people," said Rita Stoermer of Schofield Women's Golf Club. "You like to win but not everybody can. Meeting people is second best."

"There are several ingredients that make this a successful golf tournament," said Michi Okinaka of Waialae, who was assistant to Penny. "I think the ingredients are competition,

fellowship and socializing. The most important is fellowship. I think it's just getting together with different golf groups."

Norm Guenther, publisher of Hawaii Golf magazine, put it this way: "The ladies seem to enjoy the social side, which doesn't mean they don't like to win. But it's a different emphasis. They're trying to gain the respect of their peers. You don't hear four-letter words out there when they're playing. They'll say, 'Oh, gee,' and come in to lunch."

This may be because the entire Waialae Women's Invitational revolves as much around the lunch as it does around golf. The theme is set six months in advance and is more critical than putting. One year the theme was Shotgun Shogun. Japanese lanterns advertising Suntory beer hung all over the place. Waiters and even the golf pros wore Japan Airlines *hapi* coats. Out on the course, the tee markers were shaped like Japanese fans. The luncheon menu featured *sushi*, *miso* soup, *teriyaki* chicken and vegetable *tempura*.

One of the ladies admitted that they have an advantage here because male golfers don't seem to possess the gift for classy decorations. The best they could do a couple of years before was pay $400 to use second hand decorations the women had designed for their Won Ton of Fun tournament. "The men used to bring dancing girls to their luncheon but they got raided," said another lady golfer dryly.

Other differences between men's and women's tournaments are small but significant. To make sure they get to the luncheon on time, the ladies don't all start from the first tee. They scatter out and each foursome starts from a different tee. It's like running the Indy 500 with each car starting from a different spot on the track. While it's a bit confusing to spectators, the drivers all get to lunch on time.

Another difference is the way the wahines liven up the course with interesting stops between holes. On both the front and the back nine were tea-and-cookie shops. Here the competitors could nibble on shortbread, chocolate brownies, *baklava* or poppy seed cakes served on silver trays.

There is also a tendency for the ladies to root for each other as well as themselves. A woman named Pokey Richardson broke 90 for the first time in her life on the first day of the tournament. That caused a celebration almost as big as the winning ceremony. Nothing had been going right for a lady approaching the final hole. Her score was in the deep freeze. When she chipped out of a sand trap to score a birdie, the other women in her foursome cheered as if she had won the Hawaiian Open.

"I think we have more fun than the men," said veteran Waialae golfer Mary Kuramoto. "Women can entertain themselves because many dance the hula and sing a wide range of tunes. I remember a tournament when we got rained out. The women didn't complain about it. They just came back to the clubhouse and had a party."

Aloha Shirts vs. PantyHose

A Dressing Down For Men

Visitors to Hawaii tend to assume that our only consideration in clothing is comfort, that we look the way we do because we don't really give it much thought. Nothing could be farther from the truth. Fashion in Hawaii is fraught with pitfalls dug by tradition, status, history, acquired taste and simple human nature. There are subtleties of dress around here that defy logic and cause strong men to gnash their teeth and weep. How else can you account for the dichotomy between aloha shirts and panty hose?

Perhaps a bit of history might help. You see, contrary to Hawaii Visitors Bureau propaganda, Hawaii was traditionally a formal place. Hawaiian ladies hopped out of their skins into muumuus the moment they went on sale at the first missionary Sunday school benefit. Hawaiian kings dressed in uniforms adorned with more gold braid and medals than Kaiser Wilhelm. And the rest of us were not far behind. When I came to Hawaii, *The Advertiser* had a dress code which required even sports writers to wear coats and ties. A teller in a bank would no more come to work in a sport shirt than he would wear a bathing suit to a wedding. The more fashionable women wore gloves while shopping downtown. Edna Mae Lawson, our society editor, wore hats in the office the size of beach umbrellas.

What finally started the trend toward informality was not a sensible desire for comfort, which came later, but lobbying by the garment industry. In those days, Hawaii's economy needed every bit of stimulus it could get and the folks who made beach wear played on that. Why wear business suits made in San Francisco, they pleaded, when you can help the local economy by wearing aloha shirts sewn by patriotic workers right here at home? Even a meticulously attired banker in pin stripes can understand that argument. The Rotary Club and the Chamber of Commerce had to take some action since the local economy was a motherhood issue second only to the Republican Party.

And so a few brave souls began to wear aloha shirts to work but only on Friday, that being the end of the week and a good time to celebrate. Aloha Friday took hold in spite of dire predictions by coat-and-tie defenders who claimed that sloppy dress would lead to sloppy behavior, that informality in the work place must inevitably result in inefficient performance while tie-wearers kept their noses to their grindstones at all times. I know what I'm talking about because I covered this evolution of the aloha shirt for decades. It was a slow, gradual thing.

Bit by bit, one by one, men in Honolulu discovered that you don't have to be uncomfortable on the job. As I recall, First Hawaiian Bank broke the formality barrier in the financial district by allowing tellers to wear aloha shirts and muumuus on Aloha Friday. Soon an executive or two was seen in an aloha shirt on, say, Tuesday. Then aloha shirts began to appear on Wednesday and Monday. Before long it was a stampede. The manager of McInerny, Honolulu's leading haberdashery, tried desperately to stave off the tide because he made more money selling suits than aloha shirts. But nobody would listen to him. The era of the aloha shirt had arrived.

The Iron Rule of Pantyhose

If my memory serves, women in Hawaii generally applauded the move toward aloha shirts which gave their men an athletic look and probably required less ironing. For this and other reasons I had always assumed that females were more flexible in the matter of fashion than men, less conservative and more willing to take a chance. It turns out that I was wrong. Women executives in Honolulu are now wearing pantyhose for the same reason that male executives wore neckties – as symbols of their status on the top rungs of the corporate ladder. And there has been absolutely no hint of a move toward Bare Legged Friday.

A Krauss Survey of ten of Honolulu's most successful female executives indicates that they were not about to remove their hose for any reason, comfort or otherwise. I was prompted to take the survey when an issue of *Glamour* magazine advised women executives looking for promotion to wear pantyhose in the summer no matter how hot the weather. "Coming to work without pantyhose in the summer is exactly analogous to a businessman wearing a short-sleeved shirt," the article said. Since the top male executives in Hawaii now wear aloha shirts to work, I felt that Hawaii's female executives might make an exception to the iron clad rule laid down by *Glamour*. Alas, it was not to be.

"I personally agree with the article," said Myrtle Lee, president of Island Holiday Tours. "I wear stockings every day. This may be putting it bluntly but a woman isn't dressed until she has her stockings on. If you're going to be an executive, you should look the part. A woman without hose is too casual, particularly in Hawaii." I asked if this attitude might change as men's attitudes have changed about coats and ties. "Possibly," said Lee. "But I can't shake the feeling that it's not going to happen soon. Women still have a hell of a fight to prove themselves. We've come a long way but image is still extremely important."

Andrea Simpson, vice president for corporate communications at Pacific Resources, said she wouldn't think of coming to work without hose because she always dresses in

suits and has a conservative background. Did she feel about hose the way men used to feel about their neckties? "No," she said firmly. "I consider ties optional. Hose are mandatory."

The only chink I found in this inflexible rule was at Amfac where women in the executive suite on Aloha Fridays could wear muumuus that cover up their legs. Toby Pontius, vice president and assistant to the president at Amfac, said she wore hose except when in a muumuu.

Ann Simpson, First Hawaiian Bank community relations officer, said she didn't wear muumuus and that hose were a must, not only for appearance but for comfort. "It's awkward getting out of a car in a muumuu," she explained. "When I put on a muumuu, I feel more casual. It's not business attire. You don't see the mayor in a muumuu (Hawaii had a woman mayor at the time)." As for pantyhose, "In her day, my mother wore a corset. Every day, I put on pantyhose. It's uncomfortable to wear shoes without hose."

Sharon Weiner, president of the public relations firm of Stryker-Weiner Associates, said she invited 45 women business executives to a tea and none came in a muumuu. "I didn't check on their pantyhose," she said. "I've worn stockings all my life. They make your legs look better."

Even women executives in Waikiki wore pantyhose. "I never go without stockings," said Patricia Offer, area sales manager at Sheraton Hawaii for Midwest U.S.A. "It's like a uniform. The only women I can think of in Waikiki who don't wear stockings are tour escorts."

The same rule applied at City Hall. Marilyn Bornhorst, city councilwoman at the time, said she went barelegged when she came back to work after raising her family but put on hose for three reasons: for smart appearance, to make her legs look better and to make her shoes more comfortable. "Almost any woman over eighteen looks better in pantyhose," she said. "They're very comfortable. You should try them sometime."

The only woman who said she did not wear hose to work was an attorney which is ironic because male attorneys were among the last to don aloha shirts in their offices. This may be because they are required to wear coats and ties in court. "I'm not known for a fashion plate," said the attorney. "I almost never wear pantyhose or nylons. Nobody in court has ever remarked on my not wearing them. I've just never thought about it."

Apparently she did after my article came out because the next time I saw her she was wearing hose.

Which Way Will We Jump?

As you can see, Hawaii is evolving one of the most complicated dress codes in the nation. My efforts to keep abreast of the latest developments have required continuing research and careful attention to detail. It was for this reason that I attended the 30th anniversary luncheon of the Downtown Improvement Association whose members include Honolulu's senior as well as junior executives. At the first luncheon in 1958, held at Wo Fat restaurant on Hotel Street, author James Michener addressed an audience dressed stiffly in coats and ties. The only women present were his wife, Mari, and a few other wives of male executives.

What a change 30 years can make!

This time the Downtown Improvement Association held its luncheon at Yong Sing Restaurant and invited mayoral candidates Frank Fasi and Marilyn Bornhorst to debate following the five course luncheon. Practically all of the men who didn't have to sit at the head table wore aloha shirts. Howard Lee, president of the Gas Co. and vice president of Pacific Resources Inc., said, "The only executives

downtown who still wear suits are at Castle & Cooke, lawyers going to court and a few real estate people. I don't even wear a coat and tie to funerals anymore."

The second big difference in the make-up of the audience was a large representation of women. And they were all dressed more formally than the men. The accounting firm of Deloitte Haskins & Sells had bought a table. All the men wore aloha shirts. The only person dressed up was Laura Matsuda, manager of one of the departments. She had on a suit outfit. "I think women in business dress better than the men," she said.

It was true. At the Hawaiian Telephone table, all of the women outdressed the men. "This is typical," said Caroline Ingersoll in international marketing and business development. "Women in Honolulu have a more Mainland, professional look than the men. I think part of it is trying to prove their status. And there's a lot of hype about dressing for the part," she said. The fellow sitting next to her said it's just the opposite for men in business: "Here, if you dress up, they think you're putting on airs." Ingersoll said she believes that once women become more confident they will relax and dress as informally as the men.

But it's not that simple. Another complication cropped up when I talked to Victor Amiel with the commercial real estate firm of Chaney Brooks & Co. He wore a coat and tie. "Commercial real estate brokers are dressing up and, you know, I think women started it," he said. "The women are dressing and the men are catching up. Some of the best dressed women in town are secretaries."

This then is the question in Hawaii's fashion future. Which way will we jump in the next 30 years of the Downtown Improvement Association? Will men dress up to the women or will women dress down to the men?

"I think women will dress down," said City Councilman Gary Gill, who didn't own a suit until his inauguration and didn't even wear shoes until the tenth grade when he traveled to Europe and lost his callouses. "Dress is a statement of power."

"I don't see women dressing down," argued City Council-woman Rene Mansho. "But it depends on the occasion. Women want to be provocative."

State Representative Sam Lee, who spent 26 years in the foreign service before he got into politics, said everybody is missing the most important point. "I want to dispel the notion that wearing an aloha shirt is dressing down," he said. "In the old days, the highest chiefs wore only the malo and were considered to be attired appropriately to their status. We are in the process of evolving a national dress that is appropriate to the weather."

Palaka, the Kamaaina Shirt

The around-the-clock, all weather uniform for men in Hawaii is now a crisp, polyester, button down aloha shirt with the tails tucked in for business appointments and important social occasions, tails out to be sporty. Such attire is appropriate for any board room, committee meeting, legislative hearing and practically every restaurant in town at any time of the day. But if a male wishes to stand out in such a gathering, if he wishes to subtly one-up his rivals, if he wishes to proclaim his undisputed standing as a native, he will wear *palaka*.

To wear palaka is to trade on the snobbery of the Island elite, an exclusive fraternity who call themselves *kamaainas* which means "children of the land." Kamaainas feel sorry for anybody who has been in Hawaii six months less than they have. One definition of a kamaaina is someone who has been in Hawaii long enough to have planted his own mango tree and is now giving them away. The badge of a male kamaaina is *palaka*. Of course, people wear palaka who don't know what it means and that is the reason for this essay.

Just to look at, palaka is simply a cotton shirt with red or blue checks, something like a table cloth in an Italian restaurant. But palaka is not Italian. It is uniquely Hawaiian with roots deep in the culture. This sturdy, cheap cloth became standard fabric for Island work clothes because it wears like iron. It was on sale in every country store. To wear palaka was to be a cowboy or a stevedore or a hoe wielder on the plantation, a man of the people.

In time there were fewer cowboys and hoe wielders and the demand for palaka went down. It disappeared from the shelves and, therefore, became desirable to people who wouldn't think of wearing palaka before. To find a plantation store that still sold palaka was marvelous, like stumbling onto a koa rocking chair. And so Liberty House and Reyn's began to once more stock palaka shirts. This is a commendable service to kamaainas but it's not the same as wearing palaka shirts sewn at Miura Store in Haleiwa.

At Miura Store in Haleiwa you can also buy a plantation lunch pail or a straw work hat. You stand in the aisle to be measured. The ladies at their sewing machines still gossip with customers. Jane writes down the measurements in a battered ledger stuffed with tattered slips of paper. It is a ritual that began in 1919 when her grandfather began sewing palaka for sale to plantation workers. Seamstress Lillian and cutter Katherine have been sewing there for about 50 years. Their mother, Osayo Miura, started sewing there when she was 14 and ended up marrying the son of the founder. And so, with your purchase of a palaka shirt at Miura Store, you get the story of what it means.

"My grandparents came from Japan to work on the plantation in 1900," said Jane, the other daughter. "My grandmother was a seamstress. I think she taught my grandfather. The store opened in 1919. My grandparents bought the house where the central at Haleiwa ran the telephone switchboard. It was hard for Japanese immigrants to get credit from a bank so they borrowed from a fund in which all their friends had contributed. People who wanted to borrow money from the fund bid on it. The system is called *tanomoshi*. It was very popular among Japanese immigrants. My grandfather added onto the store in 1924. Since then we haven't changed anything."

Jane said her grandparents sewed lunch bags and work clothes of denim and palaka. The store sold dry goods and grandmother Miura made dresses to order, especially *holokus* or fitted Hawaiian gowns. The first years were hard because a flu epidemic in 1919 caused many deaths. In 1920 a strike by Japanese plantation workers stopped their wages. "My grandparents were overloaded with credit," said Jane. "Workers were thrown out of their houses on the plantation. They slept on the floor of the store. My grandfather drove a hack and translated in the Waialua courthouse to make extra money."

The Singer sewing machines date from 1926. In the 1930s, Jane's father and mother took over the business. He specialized in making suits to order. Later, the foot pedal sewing machines were powered by electricity. "But they're still the same machines," said Jane. So are the old, hand made sewing tables and the Japanese ruler and the lump of lead for pounding down hem joints of heavy denim and palaka.

During World War II, the Miuras turned out military uniforms. Now the store has gone full circle and is specializing again in palaka and denim. But no longer for plantation workers. Tourists from all over the world wander in to buy jeans and swimming trunks and aloha shirts.

The Ladies In Black

There is a rule of thumb that can assist you in coping with the complexity of fashion and everything else in Hawaii. At least, you might avoid making stupid comments. Always remember, WHAT APPEARS TO BE IS NOT NECESSARILY AS YOU THINK IT IS. For example, the boss is not necessarily the fellow in a coat and tie. That's most likely his public relations assistant. Getting to a party precisely on time may not be the height of courtesy because you might find the hostess still in the bathtub.

The same rule applies to the Kaahumanu Society, a bevy of elegantly black-gowned ladies who ride sedately down Kalakaua Avenue in the Kamehameha Parade. They used to walk but some of them are getting along in years. They still wear somber black broken only by vivid yellow leis. Black dresses. Black shoes. Black gloves. Black hats. To note the presence of the Kaahumanu Society at a social occasion is to know that it is one of historical Hawaiian significance.

For the Kaahumanu Society honors the greatest Hawaiian female of them all, the favorite wife of Kamehameha, champion surfer, vivacious companion, reported by Captain George Vancouver in the 1790s to be one of the most beautiful women of her time. She was also willful. After the great chief died, she led Hawaii's first women's liberation movement which overthrew the *kapus* that denied females, among other things, the eating of choicest foods such as pork and bananas. Later she held the reins of government in her capable hands with a will of iron. The ladies of the Kaahumanu Society wear black in her memory.

There is little indication that beneath the somber, funereal color lurks a pixie impulse to rebel, an irrepressible urge to kick over the traces of formality and convention. Yet it's true. One of the best keep secrets in Hawaii is that the reputation of the Kaahumanu Society is a carefully maintained front. The ladies are not sober sided at all.

I learned this in 1987 when they attended a reception to celebrate the publication of a book about Queen Kaahumanu. There they sat on folding chairs, row after row, in forbidding black, or stood at a counter daintily sipping fruit punch. Yet, on closer look there was a hint of panache, something out of kilter with funereal black, a subtle expression of humor. It finally came to me that it was done with hats. Careful questioning confirmed this.

Alice Meyer was a good example. In her black lace gown and black picture hat with ostrich plumes, she looked like Princess Kaiulani would if she'd grown up to be a grandmother. Well, the truth was that the hat came from a Goodwill store in Gardena, California during a Halloween sale. It cost exactly two bits. Alice said she bought the plumes for 75 cents apiece in San Diego in 1955.

Then there was the elegant, rakish fedora that Ann Kaapana wore. It was decorated with an ostrich feather like something out of *Vogue* magazine. But that hat had never been near *Vogue* magazine. It was an old lauhala that Ann's husband sprayed with a can of black paint from City Mill to give it that sophisticated, shiny look. Dora "Momi" Bright had on a stylish, jaunty creation of suede swathed in black lace. But the hat's pedigree is no more Hawaiian than the Goodwill picture hat. Momi bought it in Texas years ago to wear for pa'u riding. The lace came from a dime store.

Several Kaahumanu ladies explained away this irreverent, do-it-yourself habit by saying the supply of black hats in stores in Hawaii is severely limited. One of the best sources for black hats is Mary Lou Kekuewa, feather instructor for more than 15 years at the Bishop Museum, who makes hats in her spare time. Her most popular model is a black bowler. "I get them from China and they're made of grass," she said. "Felt is too heavy for Hawaii."

The hats come in all sizes and shapes. Hilda Crabbe wore a derby, Lei Girelli a silk top hat smothered in a cloth lei and an ostrich feather. The most spectacular hat belonged to Evelyn P. Medeiros. It looked like a flying saucer. "I love hats," said Evelyn. "I have twelve black hats. It must have started with my grandfather who was caretaker of the Old Pali Road. Every time a cart or a banana wagon went over the Pali, he doffed his hat. So they called him *Hemo* (take off) *Papale* (hat). My mother had many hats, one for each dress. My favorite when I was a little girl was her alligator hat. It went with her alligator shoes and alligator purse. It was green and very hot."

Lauhala Hat Weavers, Endangered Species

There was a time when one could identify a local male by the style of his hat woven from the limber and durable fronds of the *hala* tree. There were cowboy hats from the cool, grassy plateau of Waimea on the Big Island. There were fishermen's hats from the parched and sunny seashore of Kailua, Kona. There were wide-brimmed planters' hats, smart Panama hats, and everyday hats for people who worked in the cane fields.

The demand for *lauhala* (leaf of the hala tree) hats kept native weavers busy and perpetuated an ancient craft. Everybody knew that the most authentic, *kamaaina*-style lauhala hats were woven by old Hawaiian *tutus* (grandmothers) in Kona. This is no longer true. For various reasons of fashion and economy, one of the busiest lauhala hat makers now lives in Honolulu. He's a Board of Water Supply engineer whose ancestors came from Japan and his name is Andrew Okada.

More than 400 of his hats are walking around Hawaii keeping acid rain, ultraviolet rays and other harmful

64

phenomena from falling on the heads of their proud wearers. He signs and numbers each hat, which makes it a one-of-a-kind original as every authentic lauhala hat should be.

Okada charges $35 to $55 per hat, cheap for a handcrafted work of art, and explains that each hat requires from 30 to 40 hours of weaving, plus the time it takes to gather and prepare the *lauhala*. This is why lauhala hat weavers have fallen on hard times. Being an engineer and good at mathematics, Andrew has it figured out to the last penny.

"What I make on a lauhala hat works out to $1.70 an hour, and that doesn't count wear and tear on my truck when I'm collecting leaves in the mountains," he said. "There's no way you can make a living weaving lauhala hats. Just to earn minimum wage you'd have to charge $75 to $90 and who is going to pay that much for a Hawaiian hat when you can buy an imitation from Taiwan for $12.50? That's why handmade crafts are mostly hobbies today. I weave when I'm watching football games on TV or when I don't have anything else to do, just something to keep my hands occupied."

Andrew said he knows of only seven other lauhala hat weavers in the islands. That is another reason the skill is dying out.

"It's hard to find somebody to teach you," he explained. "I learned a lot on my own. When I was a boy, we lived in Lahaina. There was a Hawaiian man who sat in front of the airport and wove coconut hats. I stood outside and watched the weaver. One day he said, 'Boy, you clean up this rubbish and I'll teach you how to weave a hat.' But he only taught me to weave the brim. Later I learned how to weave the crown.

"We had a big lauhala mat in the house and a *hala* tree outside. My mother prepared the leaves and repaired worn patches in the mat. She taught me to do that. When the pineapple cannery in Lahaina closed in 1962, we moved to Honolulu. I graduated from Roosevelt High School and took engineering at the University of Hawaii but I wove coconut hats for May Day and church benefits."

Finally, Andrew made up his mind to learn how to weave lauhala hats which are to coconuts hats what mink is to rabbit. The only teacher he could find was a lady named Gladys Grace in Kaimuki back of Diamond Head. She charged $25 for as long as it took to learn.

"I don't have much time," he told her. "You just show me the first lesson in a few minutes. I'll practice and come back to learn some more." He said he quickly mastered the first lesson, making the corners at the top where the hat weaving begins. He spent another half an hour with the teacher learning how to weave down to the string line. Then he went home and made a hat.

"You don't have to pay me because I didn't teach you anything," Gladys told him. So, in payment, he showed her how to weave lauhala good luck cranes and grasshoppers. The best place to acquire one of Andrew's lauhala hat originals is at one of the craft fairs put on by the Mission Houses down King Street from Iolani Palace.

Curse of the Gulping Gulch

There was a time before Captain Cook when everybody in Hawaii believed in ghosts. Each person carried with him his or her own *mana*, spiritual force. There were spirits in the stones. Thunder and lightning spoke for the gods. The island of Molokai was known for its powerful sorcerers. But only some spirits were evil. *Kahunas Lapaau*, the healers, called upon benevolent spirits to cure the sick. Each extended family could call upon its own *aumakua*, or family god, in time of need. Thus, if your aumakua was the shark, you need never fear sharks for they were your relatives.

Missionaries, who preached the superiority of Jehovah, did their best to exorcise Hawaii of competing spirits. They registered considerable success partly because sailors had been flaunting the old *kapus* for years and Hawaiians had begun to doubt the power of their ancient gods. But Hawaiian ghosts still appear to some people and things happen now and then, even amidst freeways and luxury resorts, that are hard to explain. Perhaps the best approach is not to try, to permit each person to believe as he or she pleases. Here's one story:

In the darkness just before dawn on an April morning in 1988, a group of construction workers carried a rock the size of a kitchen chair to the top of a hill overlooking the new Waimanalo Gulch Landfill out by Nanakuli on the island of Oahu. "Hurry, hurry, before the sun comes up," said the woman directing the strange procession.

Panting with exertion, the men gently placed the rock in a nest of boulders so that it faces east, overlooking the valley with a superb view of the freeway below and the shaggy palm trees of picturesque West Beach coastline in the distance. That much of the story you can check for yourself. The rock is there at the end of a Hawaiian Electric Company service road to one of its relay stations at the top of the hill.

For the rest of it, all I can do is pass along what the workers told me about a gulch where tools disappeared and where a kiawe tree turned a somersault and a truck flipped over down the mountain. The workers refused to be quoted by name. Yet the stories circulated around Honolulu. At least, this is a first hand account from their own lips.

Work on the new landfill for rubbish began in June of 1987. The place is called Waimanalo Gulch. A desolate wilderness in our time and now Oahu's newest rubbish dump, it was inhabited at the time of Kamehameha. Kuwahine, the wife of High Chief Kalanimoku, hid there after her husband beat her for sleeping with another man. Kalanimoku ordered an island-wide search and, when he found her, decreed that the entire village where she had hidden be burned to the ground as an example to disobedient wives. This is written in John Papa Ii's *Fragments of Hawaiian History.*

"We've been having funny things happen," said one of the men working on the site of the new land fill. "Unnatural things. In one case, a man was standing on a flat rock and the thing threw him over. All of a sudden, it just flipped over." There was the acrobatic kiawe tree. A backhoe was employed to knock these wild trees down. Since kiawe trees have shallow roots, they normally simply fall over when pushed hard enough. But one of the trees jumped up and did a somersault.

"That's the same backhoe that blew a hydraulic hose," said the worker. "We fixed it. The hose blew again. We fixed it again. And the radiator hose blew." I suggested that it is not unusual for a machine to blow a hose on a tough construction job. "Not like that," he said.

He told about a payloader that was filling in a huge hole where a $17,000 fiberglass fuel tank was to be buried. The payloader pushed dirt down over the tank to cover it up. During this operation, the driver put his machine in reverse but it jumped forward and leaped into the hole, demolishing the tank. Our newspaper photographer took a picture of the smashed tank. "You're sure the driver didn't get the gears mixed up?" I asked. The worker said the gear shift was still in reverse when it hit the bottom of the hole.

About a week before we got there, a truck flipped off the service road and rolled down the mountain while a crew was blasting. True, the driver was backing down the hill on the narrow road and was in a hurry to escape the blast. Still, the workers said the accident was very unusual. Tools have disappeared, they said. A huge payloader couldn't budge a stone that had to be moved. The men dug a hole and let the stone roll down into it. The next morning, the stone was gone. That's what the workers said.

So they finally called in a Hawaiian woman recommended for lifting curses and banishing evil spirits. She said the trouble was caused by a certain stone, the "chief of the valley," which had been knocked on his side. The men quickly set the stone upright. But they got it upsidedown by mistake. Things went from bad to worse. The woman had to come out again. She recommended that they place the stone on the hill where it will not be covered by rubbish. And there it is today, an old rock with dried ti leaves at its base. I gave it a quarter just to be on the safe side.

The Ghosts of Kaanapali Beach

It is common knowledge that not everybody is privileged to see ghosts. I confess to this particular blind side. While I understand rocks, as you will see in due time, ghosts elude me. I spent one very cold night on the lava during the eruption of Kilauea Iki on the island of Hawaii in the 1950s hoping to catch a glimpse of the famous Ghost of the Saddle Road reported cavorting on this lonely stretch of highway. All I caught was a sore throat.

But there are people to whom ghosts appear as readily as Girl Scouts selling cookies. If you are one of these, and would like to strike up an acquaintance with a Hawaiian ghost, I would recommend getting a job at the utterly enchanting Kaanapali Beach near Lahaina on Maui. Understand, I cannot guarantee the appearance of a real, dead ghost. There are people who have worked at Kaanapali for years without one sighting. For other workers, Kaanapali is the ghost capital of Hawaii.

One ghost haunts elevators. Another strolls the beach at midnight. The most picturesque ghost is a Hawaiian warrior in a calabash helmet who stands guard in front of a luxurious beach cottage.

All the evidence indicates that the ghosts of Kaanapali are restless but friendly. They've never hurt anybody. They seem to congregate around Black Rock, the point of lava where souls of ancient Hawaiians once jumped off into the spirit world after death. Maybe they still do. Anyway, the ghosts appear at night and, so far, mostly to workers.

However, four guests, two couples, did once decide to go skinny dipping by the light of the moon. One of the women looked up and saw a man pushing a woman off Black Rock into the water. The tourists called the police. They couldn't find a body. A night watchman solved the mystery. He explained, as if it was common knowledge, that the man and the woman on Black Rock are ghosts and that he's always pushing her off.

A new security guard said he saw an older Hawaiian woman walk along the beach toward Black Rock one night. Thinking she might be in trouble, he followed her. At Black

Rock she disappeared into thin air. He ran to another night security guard and reported the incident, asking for help to find her. "Don't worry," said his friend. "She's just a ghost. I've seen her plenty of times."

Night switchboard operators in one of the hotels report that, now and then, a warning light will blink on, indicating that somebody has picked up the emergency phone in an elevator. This means trouble. The operator immediately calls security to check the elevator. A guard runs to the elevator. But when it arrives, it's empty. And a check of the phone inside shows there's nothing wrong with it.

A night worker at the front desk said she once took a call at about 10:30 P. M. from a guest who reported that somebody was thumping on the floor in the room above. The hotel clerk checked her listing for the room above the complaining guest. The room was listed as empty. The maid who took care of the room had died that day. None of the other maids wanted to go near that floor.

Night maintenance workers at another hotel say there's a Hawaiian warrior who guards one of the beach cottages. He stands motionless, his arms crossed. He wears a calabash helmet with streamers of tapa hanging from the bottom edge. One theory that might explain the ghosts is that the night hotel workers don't have much to do in the wee hours of the morning so they play tricks on each other to keep from getting bored.

A room that had been a disco seemed to attract the most aggressive ghosts. A member of the front desk crew went there one night to relax for a few minutes and to play the piano stored there. He put his walkie-talkie and duffle bag on the piano, then very softly played *Kanaka Wai Wai*, an old Hawaiian tune. Suddenly, the walkie-talkie jumped off the piano. Then his duffle bag hopped off to fall on the floor. He thought it was the vibration until a chandelier crashed to the floor behind him.

He rushed into the kitchen where a utility worker said, "You look like you've seen a ghost."

My Family Aumakua

For some reason, I am attracted to rocks and vice versa. I have no idea why this is so. Rocks and I get along very well. They do nice things for me. At least, that's the way it appears. Sometimes it's hard to be sure about such things. Take the old belief about picking *ohia* blossoms. *Ohia* is a wonderfully gnarled and artistic tree that grows in volcano country. It has a red, pompom blossom called lehua. *Kamaainas* at the volcano will tell you that, if you pick a *lehua* blossom, it will rain. Since it rains frequently and without effort at the volcano, the chances are at least fifty-fifty that you can make it rain by picking a *lehua* blossom.

Another example is a Hawaiian blessing. There are several. Everybody knows that a slight sprinkle during some celebration – a funeral, wedding, ground-breaking, inaugural, etc. – is a sign that the gods approve. The truth is that it sprinkles a lot around here. Sometimes it sprinkles on one side of the street and not the other. Nevertheless, everybody feels good when it sprinkles on their parade and they nod happily and tell themselves they've been blessed. A rainbow on such an occasion is an even more dramatic signal of godly approval. Since rainbows usually appear during or after sprinkles, it follows that they are rather common in Aloha Land. Yet, I always feel much better if a rainbow arches over my celebration.

Rocks are something like that with me. But not with everyone. Many modern Hawaiians warn you not to fool around with rocks. They will cause you bad luck. A case in point, again at the volcano on the Big Island of Hawaii, is the well known curse of Pele, the volcano goddess, upon anyone who picks *ohelo* berries or takes a rock from her sacred precincts without permission. Since lava rocks make inexpensive and unusual souvenirs to take home, tourists frequently pick up a couple at the volcano crater and secretly stow them in their luggage. That is why the National Park Service at the volcano has been inundated with rocks mailed back by visitors who have been hounded by misfortune on return from Hawaii. They report sickness, falls from ladders, auto accidents, marital troubles and all sorts of unpleasant happenings. After a while, they remember the volcano rocks they brought home and hastily send them back.

Was the bad luck caused by the rock or by the natural course of events? Who knows. In any event, the park rangers receive so many rocks in the mail that they no longer return them to the crater but simply dump them out the back door. My experience has been just the opposite of the unlucky tourists. I've even eaten *ohelo* berries at the crater without dire consequences. However, I always ask Pele's permission first and later thank her for her generosity. I treat rocks with the same confidence and respect and have found them to be good friends.

My favorite rock comes from the south end of Kealakekua Bay where Captain Cook was killed. The Krausses were staying there on vacation in 1963 and I was prowling through the *kiawe* thickets looking for Hawaiian ruins when I came out on a rocky shore and there was this wonderful rock of porous black lava. It stared up at me with bulging brows, eroded holes for eyes and a great lava bubble for a mouth. The features were not carved by man but are the work of nature. I had never seen a rock with such a powerful personality. It seemed lonely there in a litter of driftwood so I lugged it to our beach cottage and had it shipped home.

We put it in the back yard against the guava tree. Friends who saw it warned me to send it back. You can tell it is no

ordinary rock and that it carries *mana*. Anyway, it seems so to me. I was proud, not afraid, of my rock. It was not long before I sold a book to a New York publisher. The Honolulu Book Shops wanted to make a display in their window so I brought some Hawaiian things, including the rock. The book did quite well and, in time, I went to pick up my artifacts. But the rock had disappeared. The store clerks couldn't even remember that it had been there.

This was very annoying. In addition, the newspaper went on strike. New York publishers were no longer interested in my books. I plodded along as best I could for five years when a friend at the Honolulu Book Shops called to say that someone had found a large rock in an old cabinet and that a clerk remembered me making a big fuss about losing one years ago. I rushed to the store and rescued my rock, took it home and displayed it prominently on the lanai right beside the front door. In short order, I got a contract from a New York book publisher.

The children immediately adopted the rock as our family *aumakua* and put it to use for controlling the weather. Pleased by so much attention, the rock cooperated magnificently. We worked up a ritual patterned after that the boys and I had found effective when swimming under the waterfall at Halawa Valley on Molokai. It's a gorgeous place, a fresh water pool overhung by an enormous black lava cliff. Verdant ti and ginger grow in profusion on the banks. The only danger is from rocks falling from the cliff. To prevent this, one places a gift to the god of the cliff – a coin or a flower – on the bank, covers it with a ti leaf and anchors it with a small rock. The gift represents the supplicant. The ti, powerful defender against evil spirits, guards against injury. The rock holds it all in place. With such insurance, you may swim without fear of being beaned by a falling rock.

Our family *aumakua* ritual, however, did not involve flowers or coins. We adopted another gift because it worked so well with Pele at the volcano. It was there that the colorful keeper of the Volcano House on the crater rim long ago discovered that she likes gin. His name was George Lycurgus and he is departed now. But I remember when he used to take a square bottle of Gilby's gin to the crater rim if his hotel occupancy rate went down because there was no eruption. He would toss the bottle into the crater and, quite often, Pele would return in a fiery eruption, bringing hordes of tourists.

We decided to try vodka with our rock and it was a wise decision. Whenever the children did not want it to rain on their school carnival, or a heavy date, they poured a libation of vodka on the rock, covered his head with a ti leaf and placed thereon a rock. And it hardly ever rained. This went on for years until the children refused to attend a school carnival without first giving the rock a drink of vodka. It made for great conversation and it provided a lot of family fun.

Then my daughter, Ginger, a senior in high school, decided she wanted to see snow. Her oldest brother, Robbin, was then living in Colorado Springs. We put her on an airplane over Christmas vacation and off she went. But a week later she called home in tears to report that the trip was a failure. There was not a flake of snow anywhere. It hadn't snowed all year. I went out to the rock and explained this disaster to him. "I realize Colorado is out of your territory," I said. "But if you could get in touch with your buddies in the Rocky Mountains and explain that Ginger has never seen snow, we'd be grateful." Two days later there was a snowfall in Colorado Springs.

This could all be coincidence, of course. But, at the very least, you have to admit that my rock has never caused us misfortune, and has given me and my family a good deal of pleasure, so long as we treat him with respect. The children are grown now and away from home so there hasn't been much for the rock to do. That is, until the Baltimore Orioles set a major league record in 1988 by losing 21 games in a row.

They tried everything to win, even an earnest request by President Ronald Reagan to "win one for the gipper." They still lost.

The managing editor of *The Advertiser* at the time was a baseball fan and he asked me if there wasn't some sort of Hawaiian blessing that might break the Orioles' jinx after losing 20 straight. I told him the only thing I could think of was my rock. On the other hand, I wasn't sure my rock played baseball or even knew how to keep score. Nevertheless, I would consult him.

That night I put some vodka on the rock and explained that the Baltimore Orioles hadn't won in games which is really more than any team should be asked to endure. The rock looked interested. Anyway, the Orioles lost the next day but, on the day after, they won their first game of the season. Apparently it takes two days for the rock to arrange long distance miracles.

The Mecca of Ancestral Spirits

All over the world, cemeteries are associated with departed spirits, usually with fear and trepidation. In Honolulu, the cemeteries that attract the bulk of these stories are Chinese, the most famous being the old Chinese Cemetery in Manoa. This is because our Chinese immigrants brought with them from the old country a firm belief in ancestor worship. Every year, the descendants celebrate Ching Ming, the annual return of ancestral spirits, a Chinese and much more colorful version of Memorial Day.

Nineteen eighty-nine was an exciting year for the ancestral spirits who returned to check up on their families in Honolulu because it marked not only the 100th anniversary of the Lin Yee Chung (Manoa Chinese Cemetery) Association but also the 200th birthday of Chinese in Hawaii. On Wednesday, April 5, the descendants greeted their ancestral spirits at the cemetery by setting off 20,000 firecrackers in their honor and serving them a five-course ambrosial banquet of fish on tofu, steamed oysters with pork and tofu, shrimps, duck eggs, and chicken and roast pig.

George C. K. Young, the suave and diplomatic president of the association, announced that this was just the beginning. He was right. The Lin Yee Chung Association closed the month of Ching Ming on Sunday, April 23 with the biggest event ever held in the historic, century-and-a-half-year-old cemetery, the mecca of ancestral spirits in Hawaii. A four piece Chinese orchestra and the Royal Hawaiian Band played, 20,000 firecrackers were set off and a 200-foot-long dragon danced in honor of the spirits of Chun Hoon, Wat Kung, Luke Chan, Y. T. Lum, Doo Wai Sing, Ching Chou, Lau Tang, Henry Awa Wong, Kim Ak Ching, Buck Hung Wong, Calvin Kee Chung Lum, Henry C. H. Chun-Hoon, Tim Kau Chow, Y. N. Lum, Jack Quon Young, Dr. Hing Biu Luke, Samuel S. Luke and many other distinguished Chinese of Hawaiian history to numerous too mention here.

Young explained that anyone is welcome to honor the ancestors during the month of Ching Ming. The appropriate foods to bring, nibble and share with the ancestors, he said, are oranges, hard boiled duck eggs and peanuts. The best place to sit is under the large banyan tree planted in 1914 by Lum Sum. This spot has a gorgeous view of the graves, tropical Manoa Valley, the high rises of Waikiki beyond and the ocean in the distance. The tree shades the great tomb of Lum Ching who found this perfect site for a cemetery in 1851 and inspired Chinese friends to buy the land.

You see, Lum Ching was a geometrician. He was able to correlate heavenly bodies, especially stars, with geographical features on earth, such as mountains and rivers, to determine their spiritual real estate value. You might call him a spiritual real estate appraiser. He could tell a client to the penny not only what the land was worth but also whether the spirits would go along with the sale. Here in Manoa, while hiking one day, he found a "dragon's pulse," a rare and lucky omen. On a bluff deep inside the valley was a marvelous view of taro patches below and fishing grounds beyond so the departed ancestors could look down and see that there was plenty of food for their descendants.

Because of Lum Ching's important contribution to the honoring of ancestors, he was moved in later years into the shade of the banyan with the best view in the cemetery. His grave was designated Tai Kung Sarn or the great "Tomb of All Departed Ancestors," white and low and broad and gracefully curved. Just to the left is a smaller white tomb honoring the Earth Mother who has generously provided such a magnificent resting place. So, you see, this spot is right in the middle of things.

It was not until 1889 that the Lin Yee Chung Association was formed with strong support from ten leading Chinese societies to operate the cemetery and otherwise make sure that the ancestors are properly honored. The association has had to solve numerous problems over its long career. For one thing, previous burials were exhumed while digging graves. Young said he thinks Hawaiians used the place as a burial ground in ancient times. Kamehameha and Kaahumanu had a house nearby. These exhumed bones were carefully kept and are now buried at the White Mound, each in an individual urn, below and to the left of the banyan tree. Although probably not Chinese, these ancestral spirits are also honored every year.

Another problem was the desire of immigrant Chinese to have their bones returned to China. However, what with lack of funds and health department regulations, Young said, some of the bones are still here. So a Bone House was built at the bottom of the cemetery. Inside are rows of crocks containing the bones of departed Chinese dating back as far as 1919, patiently awaiting return to their homeland.

Young visits the grave of his parents regularly because the honoring of ancestors is a demonstration of piety. However, his wife feels better if he puts a green onion in his back pocket before he goes to the cemetery. Green onions ward off evil spirits. When he was a boy, he said, his mother did not let him swim or climb cliffs during Ching Ming because one of the returned ancestral spirits could have a grudge against him and knock him off the cliff or push his head under water. You might keep this in mind during April.

How Spiders Saved the Baby Jesus

Hawaii's immigrants come from so many places in the world that our religious customs provide fascinating glimpses into the cultures of other people. More than that, customs brought by immigrants as long as a century ago and adapted to life in the plantation camps have become frozen in time. So they are found nowhere else in the world.

That's how it is with the Portuguese *lapinha* or nativity scene of Eleanor Souza O'Day who lives on Kalanianaole Highway out by Aina Haina. Every year she sets up the elaborate stepped scaffold to display her array of statuettes, dishes, sprouting wheat, fruit, nuts and ceramic candle holders that are placed just the way she was taught as a girl. Eleanor remembers very clearly the Christmas many years ago when she did not put on the chestnuts the way she was taught by her godmother. This redoubtable lady, 89-year-old Mary DaMatta, placed her hands on her hips, glared at her goddaughter and said severely, "You no put, I no teach."

"But *madrinha* (godmother)," said Eleanor, "my mother said poor people didn't put chestnuts on the lapinha. They're $4 a pound. She said they were so expensive that in her family they ate them."

"I no eat, I PUT!" declared Madrinha Mary.

And so every Christmas, just as her madrinha taught her, Eleanor puts half a dozen chestnuts in a semicircle around the statue of the Christ Child that her father brought from the Azores in steerage aboard the steamer *Hansa* in 1882.

"My father's Christ Child is bigger even than the one in the Portuguese collection at the Bishop Museum," explained Eleanor proudly. "My grandfather was a peddler so he could get statues cheap. Farmers couldn't afford such an expensive Christ Child. Every Christmas my mother bathed him in wine with a piece of cotton. We children were not allowed to look because the Christ Child has a little penis. I have made pants for him to wear under his robe."

Eleanor said she did not realize that her nativity scene is one of a kind until she went to her homeland in 1978. "I wanted to trace my ancestors so I went back to the Azores," she said. "I took along a picture of my lapinha. They said they had never seen one like it. This one comes from 100 years ago on the plantation. It hasn't changed in all that time."

Eleanor said the lapinha is so much work to put up every year that her daughter has decided not to continue the tradition. So the lapinha will be donated to the Honolulu Academy of Arts. To preserve the Portuguese legends passed down in her family that go with every piece, Eleanor has written them down.

"My mother told me her father gathered the children in a circle on Christmas Eve," Eleanor said. "He read the Christmas story from the Bible and told the children Portuguese legends that go with it. Like the wheat. When the Holy Family was fleeing from Bethlehem they saw some soldiers in the distance. They hid in a wheat field and left a path of crushed wheat leading right to them.

"The spiders in the wheat knew the soldiers would find the Baby Jesus so they spun cobwebs across the path of the Holy Family. The soldiers stopped and said, 'No one is hiding there because the spider webs are unbroken.' They continued on and the Baby Jesus was saved. My mother said her father tickled the children to show how the spiders spun their webs. She said she always sat right next to her father on Christmas Eve because she liked to have him tickle her."

To commemorate the legend, Eleanor puts dishes of wheat growing like alfalfa sprouts on the lapinha. She gets the wheat at a health food store. The lapinha should also have peas and corn, she said, but the seeds are available only at feed stores where they are treated chemically and won't sprout.

"Anyway, I don't know any legends about the corn and the peas," said Eleanor. "But I have rosemary growing outside because Mother Mary hung clothes to dry on rosemary bushes on the way to Egypt. She also bathed the Baby Jesus in rosemary water because it's oily. My mother used to give my father strong rosemary water instead of castor oil when he was constipated."

Voyage of *Hokule'a*

The godfather of adventure writing in the Pacific is William Dampier, an English buccaneer born in 1651, whose journals became the model for adventure-travel books. His accounts of slogging through the jungles of Panama or trading broadsides with Spanish galleons off the Pacific Coast of South America revolutionized the way authors told such stories and started a new literary genre.

One book of Dampier's adventures influenced Jonathan Swift in the writing of *Gulliver's Travels*. The idea for *Robinson Crusoe* came to Daniel Defoe after reading Dampier's account of his rescue of a castaway seaman named Alexander Selkirk at the Juan Fernandez Islands in the Pacific.

After Dampier, the logs of explorers became best sellers around the world. For a century the Pacific voyages of George Anson, James Cook, William Bligh, Louis Antoine de Bougainville, George Vancouver and many others enthralled armchair adventurers and inspired yachtsmen for another century to go adventuring among the South Sea Islands.

There is another genre of Pacific adventure stories less well known although even more exciting, the legends of Polynesians who sailed the vast Pacific a thousand years before Europeans ventured there. These legends motivated a group of young Hawaiians in the 1970s to build a 60-foot-long replica of a double-hulled voyaging canoe of the type that, according to legend, brought the first settlers to Hawaii. The canoe is called *Hokule'a*.

But quite a few anthropologists insisted that a stone age people with no knowledge of the compass, sextant or other navigational aids were incapable of making purposeful voyages in primitive outrigger canoes. The discovery of Hawaii and other Pacific Islands, therefore, must have been accidental. The legends must be wrong. And so the builders of *Hokule'a*,

a group calling themselves the Polynesian Voyaging Society, went avoyaging to prove that the legends were right.

Since the art of non-instrument navigation was utterly lost in Hawaii, they enlisted the aid of a short, brown-skinned man named Mau Piailug who hails from the remote atoll of Satawal in Micronesia where sailors still find their way at sea by the stars and the swells. Mau navigated the *Hokule'a* with her part-Hawaiian crew from Honolulu to Tahiti in 1976, demonstrating that it is possible to make this voyage without either compass or sextant.

Then he took a pupil, Nainoa Thompson of Honolulu, who memorized Mau's star compass and trained himself in steering by the direction of the swells. In 1980, Nainoa navigated *Hokule'a* again to Tahiti with Mau along to give advice. Again the canoe made a perfect landfall. But the Hawaiian voyagers were not satisfied. In 1985 they set out on a two-year, 12,000-mile voyage to retrace the major migration routes of their ancestors all over the Pacific. On a short leg of this voyage, they invited me along.

At last, I had my chance to write adventure in the tradition of not only William Dampier but of the old Polynesians as well. I'll begin my account on the island of Moorea about twelve miles off Tahiti, the capitol of French Polynesia. It was here that my shipmates and myself were guests of a Tahitian cultural group in a tropical compound of grass thatched buildings. We ate a feast in the meeting house, then retired to sleeping houses.

I awoke on a mattress in the Tahitian *fale* (house) in the dark to the soft, musical tone of a conch shell. Mel Paoa of Molokai stood over me, an indistinct shadow against the dim flame of a kerosene lantern. "It's four o'clock," he murmured. "Time to get up for the fire-walking ceremony."

A Tahitian woman padded through the open door to graciously give each of us a white *pareu* (wrap-around) and a coconut leaf lei. This was not something I looked forward to, walking on hot stones in the dark. But *Hokule'a* stirred a strong cord of ancient tradition in the hearts of Polynesians.

Fire walking, the rite of purification, had not been performed on Moorea for at least 50 years, according to Tupapaurau, leading orator of the island. He was 60 years old and did not remember a performance.

"We have revivied the ceremony in honor of *Hokule'a*," explained Gabriele Carlson, a researcher of traditional history at Tahiti's museum, T-Ana-Vaha-Rau. She said Moorea wanted the honor of purifying the Hawaiian crew for entry into the great *marae* (temple) of Taputapuatea on the island of Raiatea (my destination). It is the Vatican of Eastern Polynesia.

So, reluctantly, I wound the *pareu* around my waist and stepped into the cool darkness outside where the moon rode high against the cliffs and clouds slid swiftly past the peak of Maua Puta. The *Hokule'a* crew, ghostlike in white *pareus*, waited in a quiet, anxious group. Tahitian women smeared us all with coconut oil for protection against the chill.

Tahitians stirred the stones heating over live coals in a pit about seven or eight feet square. Tave, a huge brown man in a ti leaf skirt, stood before the pit. He held a large bunch of fresh ti leaves; he was the *kahuna* of the fire walk. Six younger Tahitians in white *pareus*, three on each side of the pit, took their stations. Tave walked to the pit with slow, heavy strides, uttering a prayer, then beat the stones with three forceful blows of the ti leaves. A rooster crowed. Four blazing torches cast a red glow against the graceful, gray trunks of coconut palms.

Tave walked slowly into the pit and strolled to the other side. He stepped out of the pit, turned deliberately and walked back across as sparks leaped from the crevices below

his feet. I was still half asleep, but awake enough to know that I had no intention of setting foot into that fire pit.

Now Tave led his whole troupe into the pit and back again. They continued to walk in and out as if it were some sort of somber parade. Next, Dr. Abraham Piianaia, the Hawaiian scholar who acted as our talking chief, stepped forward with the entire crew of *Hokule'a* at his heels. Good grief, they were going to walk across the stones. I was too much of a coward to be left behind. There was no choice but to jump into the line.

I was last, just ahead of Tupapaurau, who ended it. There was no time to think. I had to hurry just to get there. So it came as a pleasant surprise to find that the stones were merely warm. Even so, I had to run across the pit in order to catch up. But the next time we walked over the stones, I strolled nonchalantly. After all my anxiety about the fire walk, I was enjoying it. For some reason, I thought of death. Probably that wouldn't be nearly as painful as I expected, either.

Canoe captain Gordon Piianaia, son of Abraham, had a different explanation. He said the importance of the fire walk is not in overcoming heat but in the act of purification. We disagreed about how hot the stones had been. Whatever their temperature, Gordon was right. The rite certainly purified me. I've never been more scared in my life.

We drank hot coffee out of coconut shell cups and munched on crisp French bread for breakfast at dawn, then lolled around to wait for the official *kava* ceremony, a Polynesian diplomatic summit meeting. Carlson said it was the first kava ceremony on Moorea since the missionaries exerted their influence in the 1790s. She said it took two weeks to find the right kind of kava in the mountain valleys for the ceremony.

Tupapaurau's opening oration explained, "We have drunk the blood of Christ in the last century, not *kava*. This (ceremony) is not to be backward but to show that we are all brothers in the Pacific Ocean." Abe Piianaia responded in Hawaiian, his eloquence matching that of Tupapaurau.

The Tahitians had called the ceremony to hear about *Hokule'a* and to learn how they could build and sail their own voyaging canoe. To explain such a complicated process in so short a time seemed impossible. But Abe solved the problem by simply introducing the crew and describing their backgrounds.

First came navigator Nainoa Thompson, only 32, yet a veteran of multiple voyages, who had studied the stars for ten years not only under Mau but in the planetarium at Bishop Museum in Honolulu. Also captain Gordon Piianaia, director of Hawaiian studies at Kamehameha Schools, a veteran in *Hokule'a* and holder of a merchant marine master's license. Next, Leon Sterling, bald first mate, a deep sea canoe voyager with thousands of miles behind him, a cabinet maker who could fix anything on board and who also held a merchant marine master's license. Finally, Mau Piailug, Nainoa's teacher, the most accomplished pathfinder and sea-farer of all who held the skills at his fingertips.

By this time the Tahitians were calling our white-haired talking chief, Papa, a term of endearment. "That is a compliment," Abe answered. "My wife will be pleased to know that I have so many children in Moorea." Everybody laughed in delight.

Although my leg of the voyage was more of an island-hopping pleasure cruise than deep sea navigation, no voyage of a double-hulled canoe between islands encircled by reefs can be made without danger. For this leg, *Hokule'a* was equipped with a 70-horsepower outboard motor. This was something like powering a 747 airliner with a rubber band. Nevertheless, the outboard provided an extra margin of safety when threading through the narrow passes of French Polynesia because we sailed when the wind was right and that was often at night.

The sun had long set when the anchor cables came in over the *manus* (upswept bows) as we hauled away under a full moon. Huahine, our next island destination, lay more than 100 miles away by our route from Moorea. Nainoa, after staying up all the night before to check the wind, had decided to leave at 9 P.M. That meant we would have to thread our way through the pass in the dark without a tow. The gendarmes, who owned the biggest power boat on Moorea, refused to risk taking it out after dark for our purpose. This pass is named *Tupapauyua*, Spirit of Death.

"I want silence on deck on the way out," said Gordon, canoe captain, as we gathered around the foremast. "Our outboard isn't too reliable. The only voice I want to hear is Nainoa's."

There were no navigational aids at Fareaitu, where we had landed to be with the Tahitians. Nainoa had arranged to have the owner of a pickup truck drive onto the jetty and switch on its lights. He lined up the truck lights with a cluster of lights on Tahiti across the channel. It was eerie going out like that. Our Tahitian friends on the jetty sang until their voices faded into the grumbling whine of our outboard.

A small *motu* (sandspit) covered with ghostly coconut palms slid by on the left. Menacing fangs of white foam appeared ahead on both sides. We moved slowly through the small opening, guided by the do-it-yourself range lights. And when we cleared the pass, there was no wind. So much for Nainoa's careful plans for catching the wind.

I had not expected that so much of our sailing would be done at night. That meant lack of sleep, even though the captain had not assigned me to a watch. I didn't have to be on duty at a particular time like most of the crew. Yet, sleep was not easy to get. The crew's quarters were cubbyholes on each side of the deck over the canoe hulls. There were cubbyholes for only half the crew, one man sleeping in each. Abe Piianaia and I were assigned to the number four starboard compartment, a cubicle the size of half a pup tent protected from the spray and rain.

It was midnight before I had a chance to turn in. Then I got up at 4 A.M. to help with the sails. It was no wonder that the men who sailed *Hokuleʻa* were in such good physical condition. Their work never stopped. Going to sea meant getting in mooring lines and anchors, then raising the gaff and boom and sail ready for setting. Setting each of the two sails was a complicated, hand-crafted operation because there were no mechanical gadgets, just rope and knots and muscle and know-how. It never seemed to go the same way twice. Even the standing rigging, which held up the masts, had to be adjusted every time we made sail, like a woman pulling down her girdle before making an entrance.

The sun came up on a cobalt blue ocean. We shut down the outboard as the wind freshened. Sea birds wheeled overhead. Nainoa had slept only in snatches on one of the navigator's platforms on the stern. Mau Piailug, his teacher, was giving him a free hand to make his own decisions. He peered anxiously ahead for Maiao, a small island 47 miles, mountain top to mountain top, from Moorea. For us to be on course, Maiao must be in a direct line with the rising sun and Moorea.

When the canoe was out of sight of land, Nainoa found his course by different means. He had learned the routes of scores of stars across the sky and the places where they rose and set. He was as familiar with the wandering path of the moon as he was with the way to the bathroom at home. During the day he used the sun. But above all, during daylight hours, he steered on the swells.

In the North Pacific, an everlasting Northeast Trade Wind drives the waves toward the southwest. In the South Pacific, the Southeast Trades sets swells toward the northwest. Changes in the direction of the swells, caused by storms or islands in their path or a veering of the wind, could be detected by Nainoa at dawn and at dusk from the position of rising and setting stars.

Mau, the old master, could feel at almost any time the dominant swell and three or four smaller swells in the seat of his pants. He was once asleep in his cubbyhole when the steersman of *Hokuleʻa* got too far off course. The change in the motion of the canoe as it rode over the swells awoke Mau. He jumped onto the deck and corrected the course. Nainoa said he was still unable to read the swells with the inbred skill of his teacher. But even *Hokuleʻa* helmsmen learned to steer by the dominant swell.

Snake Ah Hee, chief cook and steersman from Lahaina, was putting out saloon pilot crackers and hot coffee for breakfast when Nainoa suddenly shouted, "Maiao, there, there!" He ran forward and scrambled up the foremast like a monkey to make sure. It was Maiao. He had been only half a mile off course. Now he could relax for a while.

For the first time he sat and talked about what he had learned about finding the pathway for voyaging canoes. Take birds, for instance. He said most of what we have read about finding islands by following homeward-bound land birds is rubbish. The only birds he had observed flying to their islands are the fairy and noddy terns. And he had seen these birds hundreds of miles out, not to a maximum of 20 miles as had been authoritatively written. Nainoa said boobies don't have to return to land. They sleep on the ocean. Frigate birds sleep in the air.

He is an amazing man and his ability to function with a few hours of sleep per day during a voyage is phenomenal. Sleep for him at sea is a luxury because his brain is the chart on which the canoe's daily positions are recorded. It's the computer that constantly registers information to keep the canoe on course. All of it has to be retained in his memory because nothing can be written down. He said his last voyage to Tahiti was his worst, bad weather all the way. If he's lucky, he gets three hours of sleep in 24 at sea. In bad weather, he gets none at all. After his voyage to Tahiti in 1980 he was unable to fall into a deep sleep for nine days.

Nainoa said we would steer on Maiao until we lost it. By then, we would pick up Huahine. The sun blazed down as the little island came into focus. I smeared suntan lotion on my arms and legs. Shade is a precious commodity on a voyaging canoe. Lack of sleep blurred everything.

I marveled at the inexhaustible energy of Leon Sterling, the first mate, with his shaved head and bushy beard. He had been up all night hauling, repairing, cleaning, shifting anchors. Sterling was always alert, always in motion, always courteous to his shipmates. There was no formal routine about the ships work. Each veteran crew member knew instinctively what had to be done. It was about as spontaneous and orderly as a *luau* (Hawaiian feast) in preparation.

I felt stupid and useless. But mostly I was just numb from lack of sleep. Snake fixed a lunch of rice and pork and beans with a little Vienna sausage, served by ourselves in steel bowls. The old Hawaiians would have eaten dried fish and taro.

I ate, then went forward to contemplate *Hokule'a's* toilet, a net stretched across the bow between the forward *manus*. This is where crew members relieved themselves into the ocean. In high seas, you spent part of your toilet under water. The waves were only moderate so I fetched my precious store of toilet paper, went to the bow and pulled down my pants. Gingerly, I crept out on the net like an insect in a spider web, and squatted. The waves pitched and splashed below. The limitless sky arched overhead. I was alone with the elements. It was like soaring over Niagra Falls in a hang glider with my pants down.

The afternoon passed slowly. I was exhausted but there was no bunk for me to sleep in because my partner, Abe, occupied our compartment. Work on the canoe never stopped. Maiao faded into the haze. We steered by the sun. Much later,

Nainoa spotted Huahine directly on target. It was so faint I looked for ten minutes before I saw the faded mountain skyline. Chad Babayan, who came from Maui and was learning navigation, called it an example of how easy it is to miss a landfall in open ocean.

A little before 5 P.M. – a guess because the last thing we did before boarding *Hokule'a* was take off our watches – Snake served hamburgers canned in gravy and mixed in the steel bowls with rice, canned corn and apple sauce. I ate and climbed into our bunk which Abe had vacated. *Hokule'a* sailed along at about six knots to a symphony of creaks and groans and squawks and grunts from the rigging. I fell into a deep sleep.

When I crawled out of my hole, it was night and the deck was moon-drenched. The black bulk of Huahine loomed above us, mysterious mountains shouldering into a star spangled sky. We were motoring through the pass at Fare without a pilot, steering on two green range lights on shore.

Fare, the port town, was fast asleep as we tied up at the ferry landing. Sacks of taro were piled under the open air pier shed. Across the main road a feeble street light shown on a frame building that carried a sign, SUPER FARE NUI. It was the local supermarket. The village lay in soft shadow. The only people awake were a young couple making love on the dock. One of our crew stumbled over them while making a line fast.

I was too tired to wonder if other Polynesian voyagers had arrived at their destinations unheralded. Probably, because they sailed like us when the wind blew, not on schedule. The sails came down and lay crumpled on deck. I curled up on the box which housed the emergency radio and went back to sleep. Crew members dropped where they stood and lay as if dead under the lowered sails, on the navigator's platforms, in the after hatches.

It was first light when my eyes opened. An old man on a bicycle wheeled silently out of the gloom to stare at this spaceship of his ancestors. He scratched his head in wonder. Two young men came silently to his side. They talked in low, wondering tones. John Kruse of Kauai, a thick stubble darking his jaw, stuck his head up. He saw the trio on the dock in the pale light, and got to his feet.

Here, then, would be the first contact between a voyaging canoe of the past and the people of Huahine who apparently didn't know it existed. I waited for this historic confrontation. Kruse waved in a friendly manner and said in English, "What time does the supermarket open?" The people of Huahine, who spoke Tahitian and French, stood mute. I pointed at the store and then at my wrist where my watch would have been. The old man held up six fingers. Captain Cook must have established communication in much the same way.

The old man rode away on his bicycle. He soon reappeared riding in the opposite direction with four loaves of French bread slung under the handlebars. Soon more people stirred, sauntering out to get French bread for breakfast, stopping to admire *Hokule'a* on the way. At 6:30 A.M. the first gaily painted jitney bus roared into town from the country to disgorge its tightly packed passengers in front of the supermarket. Two women set up a fruit stand.

A crowd gathered on the dock to stare at *Hokule'a*. Pauniu, one of our Tahitian crew, was born in Huahine. His brother invited us to use his house, two blocks from the dock, as our motel. Our sleeping mats covered every inch of floor space. Back at the dock, a school teacher brought her first grade class to admire the voyaging canoe. She was quite attractive and very French and several of the crew tried to be helpful.

Invitations came for a feast and afternoon swim across the island at the luxury Huahine Beach Hotel. We all piled into autos and pickup trucks. Still groggy from lack of sleep, I enjoyed the festivities, then went to our house at Fare to write and rest. The next day we were guests of jovial Pierre Colombani, great-grandson of a Corsican who came to Huahine in 1874 and married a Tahitian princess. Colombani owned a picturesque inn just down the street from the supermarket. His generosity earned him an invitation on board *Hokule'a* the next day for the short voyage to Raiatea.

The sail required only a few hours but for me it was a journey into remote time. We were bound for Te Ava Ma'o, The Sacred Pass, through which voyaging canoes sailed from the legendary homeland of Hawaiki. Nobody knows where Hawaiki is. It is the Garden of Eden of the Polynesians. Legends place it at Raiatea, the ancient religious capital of the Tahitians. And the legends say that voyaging canoes set sail from the great marae out through the sacred pass to Hawaii, to Rarotonga, to New Zealand.

Nainoa said old Tahitians were furious when *Hokule'a* went to Raiatea in 1976 but did not approach through the sacred pass. The canoe went to the port town instead. This time we were ready. It was for this reason we had been purified by fire. For this reason we carried gifts given us during the kava ceremony. The gifts were heavy with *mana* (spiritual power) that would propitiate the ancient gods of Taputapuatea, the most sacred *marae* in this part of the world.

We had been told at Moorea that no voyaging canoe had returned through the pass from a voyage of discovery since ancient times. We were returning from Hawaii. We had on board Karim Tauavahiani Cowan, a bronzed young Tahitian who had graduated from Damien High School in Honolulu, and for whom this voyage was a lifelong dream. For me it was an experience so uncanny it still gives me goose bumps.

My entire time on Hokule'a, except for night time sailing, had been under a warm Tahitian sky. Our voyage from Huahine began under a heavy overcast. Huahine's green-robed peaks were shrouded in mist. A rain squall blotted out Riatea across the channel. It was the kind of gloomy weather Hawaiians believe is a sign the gods are in attendance, an omen of an important event.

"It's unusual for us," said Raiatea resident Tom Cummings later. He is part of the Kauai Cummings clan in Hawaii. "We've had three weeks of sunshine. The weather report said it would be clear. Then, on the day *Hokule'a* arrived, it began to cloud up."

As we moved out of the channel at Fare, I noticed the foot of a rainbow to the right. The other foot showed below the overcast to the left. We were beginning our voyage by sailing under a rainbow. There is no more auspicious omen in all of Polynesia. Maybe that's why I felt good in spite of the rain. Maybe it was the two-day stay on laid-back Huahine where I caught up on my sleep. Maybe it was the anticipation of seeing at last the most famous *marae* in Polynesia. Maybe it was the rainbow. Anyway, I felt in excellent spirits.

The sun tried to peek out. A strong northeast wind sent *Hokule'a* flying. That might have been why I felt so good. It's exhilarating to bowl along in a brisk, fresh breeze on the open deck of a graceful canoe. Karim stood at the bow, like an etching of a Polynesian voyager, peering into the mist ahead. I climbed into the port side navigator's platform to photograph the picturesque set of the sails and scenes of activity on deck. Nainoa squatted by the rail amidships. I got him in the viewfinder and noticed a piece of the rainbow arching over his head. Another rainbow had formed, this time to starboard, over Taputapuatea. By this time everybody on the canoe was talking about the rainbows.

"My grandmother's land is next to Taputapuatea," Karim told me. "She said when you go through the pass if you see a rainbow it is good luck. When you go through, strange things will happen that not all the people understand. A lot of things will be lift up. There is so much *mana*."

Now Raiatea showed clearly ahead, half hidden by clearing mist, a long, mysterious lizard of an island. I looked down at the steering paddle. It was lashed to the deck. "Hey," I said

to Leon Sterling, "who's steering this canoe?" He explained that on certain points of the wind the canoe can be steered by the trim of her sails. Nobody had touched the paddle since the sails were set. We were dead on course. A little later I heard Nainoa mutter to himself, "She's taking herself straight to the pass."

We went through and anchored in the shallow lagoon. The people of Raiatea clustered on a small *marae* at the shore under towering coconut trees with ghostly gray trunks. This was one of two small marae on the beach, flanking the great *marae* inland. One of the small marae is for the famous demigod Maui who sailed away, the other is for a brother who stayed on Raiatea. The delegation from Moorea brought out a boat that ferried us to the beach.

There the people draped us with leis, greeted us with oratory and gave us a concert of songs sung in wierd harmony and a strange rhythm that was wild and provocative. But they did not take us to the marae. Our welcome was performed on the beach. Then they went home, their duty done to the visitors from Hawaii.

Only then did we make our own way past an upright monolith hoary with age to the great, open courtyard paved with flagstones. Huge upright slabs formed a wall higher than a man's head at one end. The setting was an eerie one and the color that sticks in my mind is gray. It may be because the coconut palms are very old, soaring on spindly trunks to great height and weathered to a ghostly gray. We squatted on the flagstones in the shadow of the stone slabs where the gods once sat, and listened to Tom Cummings tell us what he knew of Taputapuatea.

By this time the sun had come out so the gods must have gone home, too. It was something of an anticlimax. Maybe they had returned that day just to honor the canoe and her voyage through the pass.

Storm in the North Pacific

There was a time when a storm at sea pitted frail humans against the cruel ocean, when a battle with the waves was a lonely experience and the sailor's only outside assistance came from God. Those were the days before satellite navigation and the Coast Guard rescue service. A storm at sea is still a terrifying experience that tests the skill and resolve of all who go down to the sea in ships. Yet the voyage of the Marr family of Long Beach, California to Hawaii in 1989 demonstrates that sailors in danger can now communicate with somebody else besides God.

Mike Marr, a mechanical engineer and a veteran yachtsman, talked his wife, Barbara, a secretary, into making a dream voyage to the South Seas. So they tuned up their 47½-foot yacht, *Makora*, took daughter Michelle Glass out of school, and set sail for the most romantic ports in the world; Tahiti, Tonga, Samoa, New Zealand, the Gilberts.

Their ordeal began two years later on the last leg when they departed Tarawa Atoll in the Gilberts, part of Kiribati near the equator, for home. They planned to sail to 40 north latitude about 1,000 miles north of Hawaii where the wind blows west. The westerlies would take them across the Pacific to North America where they would coast down in the trade wind to Long Beach.

"But at 40 north, we got only three days of west wind," said Barbara. "Ninety-eight percent of the time there was no wind, too much wind or wind from the wrong direction. It blew up to 60 knots."

So the boat went backward as often as it went forward. What was to be a pleasant cruise of three weeks turned into three frightening months. "I was scared and it's not because I'm a kid," said 17-year-old Michelle. The sea was so rough that the family could not go on deck for days at a time. The wind blew so hard that the yacht remained heeled over at 40 degrees for up to 36 hours. Waves came completely over the deck house, making it dark inside.

It was so wet in the cabin that the only way to dry clothes was to wear them to bed, a trick sailors used a century before while rounding Cape Horn. "At 40 degrees north latitude, you can't hang laundry out to dry," Michelle explained. "It's too cold and wet." There was no heat in the boat and the voyage took place in winter.

After about two months of making 22 miles a day in the right direction, they gave up trying to reach California. "We were 2,000 miles from Los Angeles and only 1,000 miles from Honolulu," said Barbara. "So we worked our way south." By this time they were entirely dependent on the wind because of a loose drive shaft.

Fortunately, both Mike and Barbara are radio ham operators and they carried a set in the *Makora*. The family credited other hams with talking them into port. "It was a tremendous help, like having a family out there," said Mike. "They patched us through to Barbara's parents about twice a week. When the automatic steering gear broke, they patched us through to the manufacturer in Tacoma, Washington where an engineer told us how to fix it."

Barbara said hams all over the world followed their epic voyage, providing weather reports and moral support. "It was like a soap opera," she said. The hams, worried that the plucky family would run out of food, notified the Coast Guard of their plight. On the day after Christmas, the Coast Guard radioed an offer to drop supplies by plane. "We didn't need them," said Barbara. "It's expensive for the Coast Guard to send out a plane. We still had dried peas and rice and noodles. You learn to be creative."

Mike said he knew they could make port even with no motor power. "I'm more scared on freeways than in a storm at sea," he said. At last off Diamond Head, 96 days out of Tarawa, in a dead calm on New Year's Eve with no power, the family accepted a tow from the Coast Guard. The battered yacht tied up at the Hawaii Yacht Club in Ala Wai Harbor at 9:30 P. M.

"I could smell the barbecued steak from outside the channel," said Barbara.

Over Manoa Falls Without a Barrel

Adventure in Hawaii is not confined to the ocean. The possibilities on land include the following:

Kauai – The highway does not extend all the way around this exotic tropical garden. One terminus winds up to the head of Waimea Canyon where there are trails down into its spectacular vistas and through the cool, upland forest in Kokee State Park. From the other end of the highway, a trail hugs the cliffs above booming surf along the Napali Coast for nine miles to the vast sweep of Kalalau Valley once inhabited by the people of old. The taro terraces are still there.

Maui – A 10,000-foot-high dormant volcano called Haleakala, House of the Sun, rises above this lusty, rambunctious island. The paved road wends its way to the summit where you have superb views of a crater big and deep enough to swallow the island of Manhattan. An even better way to see this magnificent wilderness, where silence sings, is to follow the foot trails. Another trail follows the parched lava shore along the backside of Haleakala. This path was built by convicts for horses in the 1800s.

Hawaii – The biggest, newest and most rugged of all the islands, Hawaii offers the greatest opportunity for adventure.

In 1973, on the 150th anniversary of a missionary expedition around the island, a group of middle aged men including myself spent 30 days retracing the historic, 300-mile route on foot, camping along the way. There are nature trails in the Volcanoes National Park winding through craters, over lava flows and amidst forests devastated by fire.

Oahu – Like Kauai, Oahu's coast highway was never completed although a railroad once took passengers and freight around the sand and lava loneliness of Kaena Point, with an open end, now closed even to motorcycles. This is a great place to escape from the city for a while from either end of the road, to smell the sea and stretch your muscles. Easy trails lead to Manoa and Sacred Falls, and harder trails lace the Koolau Mountains.

You can buy books that describe hikes on all of the islands. Most of them are safe and don't require the conditioning of an Olympic athlete. The hike to Manoa Falls, for example, is a Sunday stroll for families with small children who picnic under the falls. But there's danger for daredevils who leave the trail to test their courage on the cliffs above the falls where the signs tell you to keep off.

In 1986, 23-year-old Jerry Cooper, Jr. of Grants Pass, Oregon discovered this for himself. He had been in Honolulu for about a month when he hiked to Manoa Falls. Cooper said he enjoyed rock climbing along the Rogue River so he and a friend climbed up to see what was above the falls. It was so much fun they went back and climbed again into a closed watershed area posted by the state Forestry Division, with violators subject to a fine of up to $500.

"I climbed Manoa Falls at least 15 times," he said. "There are eight more falls higher up. Three of us went up on Thursday, July 24, at about 3 P.M." Cooper said he was crossing the stream above the falls when his feet slipped out from under him. He slid into a shallow pool and went over the edge of the falls.

"I think I went over backwards because I was trying to grab hold of something," he said. "It happened so quick and colorful. All the colors were very bright. I must have turned around in the air. I looked down and I thought I was going to die. I knew it. Halfway down, I blacked out. The next thing I knew, my friend, Sam, was telling me to keep awake. Then I heard the props of a helicopter and, after that, I was in the hospital."

Cooper fell 125 feet into eight inches of water. A veteran at the police department said he doesn't know anybody else who has survived a trip over the top of Manoa Falls, a 12-story drop. At least three persons have been killed climbing above Manoa Falls since 1970. One fireman lost his life while rescuing a stranded hiker.

Cooper broke both ankles and his left arm, punctured an ear drum, suffered small cuts under his chin and on the top of his head, and got a black left eye. His nurse told him, "what a lucky young man he is" because he not only lived but broke no bones in his spine. "The problem was that I had my tennis shoes on, not my climbing shoes," he said from his hospital bed. "I lucked out. I had a guardian angel with me and I'm thankful."

The Pinnacle of Achievement

The major difficulty for folks who go adventuring these days is not so much a lack of grit and stamina as a dwindling arena of opportunity. There just aren't any more places where somebody hasn't been there first. All the islands in the Pacific have already been discovered. The mountain peaks have been conquered. In fact, you have to make a reservation to climb Mount Everest because there's a five year waiting list.

Consider what this means to a dedicated mountain climber like Bob Failing, a modest fellow who works at the Department of Pathology at California's Santa Barbara Cottage Hospital. At age 63 in 1989 he had no dreams of greatness although he had scaled some of the most challenging peaks in the world. But everybody else was doing the same thing so what else is new. Two hundred seekers of adventure had already been to the top of Mount Everest.

Then Failing read an article in the newspaper about another ordinary mortal who was only the seventh person in the entire world to climb the highest point in each of the 50 states. This set the doctor to thinking. He had already climbed 13 highest state points including the most difficult: Mount McKinley in Alaska, Mount Rainier in Washington, Gannett Peak in Wyoming and Granite Peak in Montana. Why should he not make history as one of the first ten people in the universe who have conquered all 50 states? Everest would have to wait.

There followed an epic mountain climbing frenzy that resulted in 37 peaks conquered in 15 months. True, the highest point in Florida is only 345 feet up and 100 feet from the nearest parking lot. The highest point in Delaware is on the double yellow line of a highway. In Iowa, it's in a pasture. But, hey, it took him 30,000 miles of air travel and 14,500 miles by auto to do it.

Failing saved the 50th State, Hawaii, for his 50th climb. He'd intended to make his historic ascent of Mauna Kea, highest point in Hawaii at 13,796 feet, on the 30th anniversary of statehood, August 29, 1989. This would make him only the ninth person in the whole world to stand at the pinnacle of achievement in all 50 states. Then he discovered that yet another seeker of immortality had scheduled a Mauna Kea climb for July 31. Failing, in spite of his effort, would slip to tenth place. That's why he moved his schedule up to July 22 when he called me from Santa Barbara and invited me along.

Frankly, I had already climbed to the top of Mauna Kea when I was much younger and there was considerably more spring in my legs. But, since there is now a road to the top, I agreed to record the event for posterity by driving to the summit in a four-wheel-drive with Larry Yungblut, Failing's brother-in-law who lives in Kona.

When word got around in the California mountain climbing fraternity that Failing was about to climax his campaign with an assault on Mauna Kea, climbing buddy Chuck Beattie of Menlo Park joined the expedition. Climber Jim Gurnham of San Francisco asked if he could come along. They showed up, loaded down with state of the art mountain climbing gear, on Friday evening at the visitor's center of Mauna Kea Observatory at the 9,000-foot level.

Understand that Mauna Kea is an enormous mound of lava and ash. The trail winds over loose cinders in an endless upward path. There are no rock faces to scale, no cliffs to conquer. So the major hazard of the climb for hikers in good condition on a nice day is sunburn. For this reason, the expedition went to bed early in preparation for a 4:40 A.M. start to avoid the sun's daytime heat. There was no hint when we rolled into our sleeping bags under a sky blazing with stars that the gods of the mountain had taken an interest in this undertaking.

Promptly at 4:30 A.M. tropical depression Eric camped right on top of us. It rained in buckets. You couldn't see across the parking lot. Rain fell in sheets. It blasted around the corner of the visitor's center where we huddled under the overhang of the lanai. The climbers would have needed bloodhounds to follow the trail in weather like that. We waited. And waited. At 6 A.M., the astronomers told us the

weather was bad all the way to the summit. Nobody was going up that day.

But Failing could not fail. He could not wait for the rain to stop. He had to be back at work on Monday. And if he abandoned his expedition, he would lose his place in history. So we set out at 7:30 A.M. in two four-wheel-drives to try and get above the rain. It just rained harder the higher we went. And harder. The windshield fogged over. We drove to 10,000 feet. It was still raining with wild abandon. Rivulets were cutting ruts in the road.

The climbers stopped for a, if you'll pardon the expression, summit meeting in the rain. I stayed in the Jeep. They reached a decision. They had come to climb Mauna Kea, by George, not ride to the top. Off they set, happily slogging through the mud, defying the elements like a mountain climber should.

At 12,000 feet, the rain turned to windblown snow. On they climbed; soaked, panting, defying the gale and having a wonderful time. Near the summit, just below the observatories, the weather cleared for about half an hour so the climbers turned off the road and made the last ascent over a sheet of new snow, switch-backing up the steep, white slope of the last cinder cone. Then the heavens opened up again. The expedition members posed for victory photos at the summit in a driving, gusting, bone-chilling downpour of snow, sleet and rain.

And so Failing became the ninth person in the universe to stand on top of all 50 states and the first to conquer the 50th State on his 50th expedition. What's more, he did it in the worst weather on Mauna Kea in July that anybody under 210 years of age can remember. Of such impossible dreams are heroes made.

Hula & Other Hawaiian Arts

A Course in *Hula* Appreciation

The Hawaiian hula has been, over the years, probably the best known and least understood of the fine arts in Hawaii. First, the missionaries condemned it to hellfire. Then tin pan alley turned it into a dance no self-respecting Hawaiian would perform. But the hula has survived these indignities to remain the heartbeat of Hawaii. As we will see, it rivals sports as a leisure activity for office workers in the islands and remains the preferred art form for increasing thousands of addicts.

It is a good idea, therefore, for those of us with two left feet, to understand what this is all about. Fortunately, one of Hawaii's most respected *kumuhula*, hula masters, John Kaha'i Topolinski, agreed to explain what's so exciting about the Hawaiian hula. He is a descendant of a legendary Polynesian navigator, a leader in the preservation of the ancient hula and a Hawaiian history teacher at Mililani High School. I explained that I would like to talk to him about the hula as I would Joe Montana about football or Governor John Waihee about politics.

What came out is more or less a hula appreciation course for people who don't dance. Here, then, are his answers to the questions you probably always wanted to ask:

"What does it take to make a good hula dancer?"

"It's a gift. Then you practice. Then it lives. I know right off the first day who has the gift. I think there is an innate sensitivity to the dance, to the involvement of the story. So that you BECOME the story. You become the warrior, the lover. It is like a spiritual experience that will touch those in the audience because it strikes in the heart."

"There are different schools of dance, say ballet and interpretive dance. Is the hula unique?"

"Of course it is. It calls upon the gods and goddesses to inhabit the dancer. Ballet doesn't do that."

"Wait a minute. When an actor is on the stage, isn't he supposed to BECOME the part he's playing?"

"Where does he get it from? Is it from his experience and training or does he call upon the gods as a hula dancer does? This concept of pleasing the gods and goddesses in the old days raised the level of excellence."

"How are you supposed to watch a hula?"

"When I see a dance, I see pictures. The chant talks about Kamehameha's battle and I see it like in a cinema. The dancer BECOMES Waialeale (the mountain) or Pele (the fire goddess). Younger *kumuhula* do this by being obvious. They streak Pele's hair with ashes and have her carry fire. That's how you can tell the traditional from the new style. One thing Kawena Pukui (a late and revered Hawaiian scholar) taught me is that it is very Hawaiian to be elusive."

"How has the hula managed to survive missionary disapproval and popularization for tourists?"

"Hawaiians may disagree on many things but when it comes to the hula they will fight for it because it contains their essence. The hula is the heartbeat of Hawaiian culture. It is the language, the history, the religion, the etiquette, the protocol. A hula master in olden times was like a little archives running around."

"But aren't there different levels of hula?"

"There is hula for all kinds of people, from classic to unrefined. So tourists are sometimes cheated because they aren't getting what the culture really is."

"Why do so many people take hula lessons?"

"I think it takes them away from their present lifestyle to one that is romantic and expressive and free from the ugliness around us. It puts them in touch with something that feels good. Hula is like a release for me."

"Everybody has a little ham in them. Is that part of it?"

"Sure it is. You must be a dramatic person to take part in any art form. Iolani Luahine (the late grand dame of the ancient hula) did it. I think Polynesians in general like to be dramatic."

"Is dancing the hula a way of becoming Hawaiian?"

"Yes. You can't dance without understanding it. Without the story, it is nothing. The chant (the story) can survive without the hula but the hula cannot survive without the chant. So when you see the hula, remember that the chanter sitting behind in the corner is the most important."

"You are credited with revival of the male hula. How did that happen?"

"As a kid I loved the hula. I liked to watch. At age nine at McKinley High School, I saw Iolani Luahine dance and it just turned me on. She was great. But I didn't dance then because of the stigma attached to male dancing. I didn't begin dancing until I was in my 30s, then it just seemed as if my ancestors had passed it on to me. It had skipped several generations.

"The popularity of male hula goes in cycles. Now it's hard to get male hula dancers again. Maybe it's because they have jobs. But I have the feeling that the hula is too demanding in an age of instant gratification. The hula is hard work."

The GTE Hawaiian Tel *Hula Halau*

Plenty of companies around the nation sponsor softball teams and bowling leagues and golf tournaments, but GTE Hawaiian Tel in Honolulu is the only business firm in the nation with its own hula troupe. We're not just talking a few free hula lessons here. This is a heavy-duty, be-on-time-twice-a-week, buy-your-own-gourd-rattles, ancient and modern, full on hula *halau* (studio or temple). In two years the dancers learned 75 different hulas from the tourist *Hukilau* to *kahiko* or traditional.

On its second birthday in 1990 the *Ho'opili GTE Hawaiian Tel hula halau* gave a benefit performance at Hana, Maui for the medical center there – three costume changes including flowers for the hair. The dressing room was a tent. The dancers collected their own flowers from back yards and cemeteries and strung their own leis.

Mamo Tamburi, customer service representative at the Pearlridge Phone Mart, said she has learned that perpetuation of the Hawaiian hula is not as glamorous as it sounds. "Try changing clothes five times in an hour with ten other dancers in a place the size of a bathroom with no air conditioning," she said. "In there are all the costumes and implements besides."

Kumuhula Maude Leina'ala Akamine recalled that her dancers have changed in a dusty storeroom at the Ward Warehouse shopping center and in a basement hallway at the Turtle Bay Hilton. At the Queen Emma Summer Palace the dressing room was a tent at the bottom of the hill. For each change, the ladies ran down to the tent, got into a different costume, ran back up the hill and tried to dance without panting. They have dressed in shopping center parking lots and at Foster Garden where there were no window blinds. The ladies hung garment bags for privacy.

But customer service rep Uilani Stone said she enjoys every minute. "I took hula years ago," she said. "As a single parent, I can't afford to pay for hula lessons. This is a good way to get back into it."

The idea for a company *hula halau* came from Akamine, an office assistant in traffic engineering. "They had a sports program, why shouldn't they have the hula?" she said. She got an okay from the Department of Human Resources and called a meeting for 4:45 P.M. on July 10 in the sixth floor conference room. Twenty-four dancers and musicians showed up, both *kanes* (men) and *wahines* (women). The rest is history.

Akamine does the choreography, teaches the dances, designs the costumes and hustles engagements. She spends twenty hours a week with the *halau* and doesn't receive a cent in return. The company pays for the costumes – nine different changes - not including ti leaf skirts which the dancers make themselves.

Dancers and musicians buy their own musical instruments and hula implements, which is only fair because the softball players buy their own shoes and gloves. On the other hand, hula implements don't come cheap. Tamburi and Stone listed their expenses:

Uli uli (gourd rattles), $50; *pu'ili* (split bamboo stick rattles), $10; *ipu*, (gourd hand drums), $35; *ka'eke'eke* (bamboo musical pipes), $45; implement bag, $25; garment bag, $50; *kukui* nut neck and wrist leis, $50; shell *leis*, $15. Akamine said her *pahu* (drum) cost $595.

All the money that comes in for performances goes out to pay for a trip once a year like the grand tour of Hana. Meanwhile, the dancers learn Hawaiian values, like getting along together. Akamine explained there is no room for temperament in the *halau*. The *kumuhula's* word is law. As on board a canoe, if you don't like the person next to you, you grit your teeth and smile. That's how you learn aloha. Out of it all comes pride of accomplishment, a sense of family and perpetuation of the culture.

The Music Man

His father named him "Robert." His wife calls him "Andy." At the Von Hamm Young Company, where he retired as president and chairman of the board, he was known as "Mr. Anderson." But music lovers know him best as R. Alex Anderson, writer of classical *hapa-haole* Hawaiian songs heard at luaus and the Kodak Hula Show for the last fifty years.

When I last interviewed him he was 94 and breaking into a new field, television. The composer of *Lovely Hula Hands, Cockeyed Mayor of Kaunakakai, Mele Kalikimaka* and more than 100 other tunes starred in a half hour special for the public television channel.

Writer-producer-director Bart Fredo said marathon interviews and shooting of about four hours of tape left him more exhausted than Anderson who held to his golfing schedule and attendance at the Rotary Club. "It started as a ten-minute segment," said Fredo. "But after I met him I knew we should do a whole show."

To commemorate the occasion I drove out to Anderson's Diamond Head mansion where he gave a relaxed interview, played his tunes on the piano and climbed three flights of stairs to show off his scrapbooks without taking a deep breath. He was in the middle of composing a tune for the 150th anniversary of Punahou School, his alma mater.

Anderson said it takes anywhere from a month to several months to complete a new song. "I do most of it in my head and I hum a lot," he explained. "When I think of a line for the lyrics, I jot it down, sometimes in the middle of the night."

Lovely Hula Hands took him about four months to write in 1940, he said. It started at a local party when Anderson was standing on the fringes while a hula dancer performed in the middle of the floor. "Aren't her hands lovely?" asked a man next to Anderson.

"That phrase really excited me," said Alex. "It described the hula so well. So I began writing a song. Meanwhile, I crewed in a yacht sailing around New Zealand. You know how sea gulls follow a boat, gliding over the water. That's where I got the phrase, 'Graceful as a bird in motion, gliding like the gulls over the ocean.' I didn't realize I had a hit. I think I gave the song to Harry Owens to play at the Royal Hawaiian Hotel. Right away it attracted attention. Then I placed it with a New York publisher."

Cockeyed Mayor of Kaunakakai, another all-time favorite, was written in 1935 after Anderson visited millionaire Paul Fagan, owner of the now-defunct San Francisco Seals baseball team, and builder of the Hana Maui Hotel.

"I was visiting Paul at his home on Diamond Head when he told me he planned to honor Warner Baxter, the leading movie star of his time, on Molokai," said Anderson. "Paul was getting up a parade at Kaunakakai with a key to the city to give Baxter as honorary mayor. Paul asked, 'Why don't you write a song about it?' So I did.

"We had dances on the Young Hotel roof in those days and the band featured the new song, then the bandleader took it back to the mainland and got me together with a New York publisher. Then it was featured in the Broadway musical, *Hellzapoppin.*"

Anderson said he was leaving his office to go home a few days before Christmas in 1950 when a secretary asked, "Why aren't there any Hawaiian Christmas songs?" He said, "That set me to thinking. I wrote a song entitled *Holiday Hula* but that never attracted too much attention. Then came *Mele Kalikimaka* and it caught on right away."

Anderson said he wrote his first song in 1912 for his graduating class at Punahou and has been doing it ever since. But song writing has always been a spare-time hobby.

"My first boss was my uncle, Conrad Von Hamm," said Anderson. "He was a strict German and didn't think much of my song writing. Once when I had a hit he called me to his office. 'Alexander,' he said in his German accent, 'I think you are not paying attention to business when you are writing music.' 'Uncle Conrad,' I said, 'it's my hobby. When you and Aunt Bernice are playing bridge, I write music.' He never brought up the subject again."

Warrior With A Brush

Koho Nakasone, a muscular five feet tall and nut brown from the sun, is an artist who has chosen Honolulu as the place to practice his art. He waits until peace descends upon Kuakini Street, where Nuuanu Valley opens into downtown, before he seeks to find the path. Then he bathes and brushes his teeth and slips into a loose, tie-around smock and baggy, drawstring pants made of blue denim like a karate outfit.

But it is not the martial arts Koho has practiced since he was eight years old, it is calligraphy, a discipline almost as athletic. Any similarity between the writing I do on my computer to compose this story and the writing he does with a wooden brush on absorbent paper in his bare living room is purely accidental.

Take the word D-R-A-G-O-N. I punch the keys and "dragon" comes out in abstract symbols like a mathematical equation. Koho swirls his brush in decisive, rhythmic strokes, moving his body like a dancer, and out comes a picture with sensuous swirls and muscular slashes. "I SEE the dragon," he said. "I can express this visually as a dragon."

He didn't actually say that because my Japanese is non-existent. His English at the time, after five years in Hawaii, was not up to the kind of ideas we were expressing. So we communicated in a kind of multidimensional language of nimble fingers, waving arms, dancing eyebrows, facial contortions and the words we had in common.

He said there is more to calligraphy than what gets down on paper. "I STROKE my words," he said. "I express myself with my body as well as the picture. Some people write calligraphy only with the brush but that is not a real art. There is no soul in the dragon."

I said, "It sounds to me as if we are talking about three dragons. There is the dragon which is the SUBJECT of your picture. There is the dragon which APPEARS in the picture. And there is the dragon IN YOUR HEAD AND BODY while you draw it. Now I ask you, which is the real dragon?"

He laughed and said, "The one that is in my head."

I told him that handwriting experts seem to agree that you can make something of a person's personality from his or her penmanship in English. He said it's the same way in calligraphy. There are six different writing techniques. On top of that, he can describe a person's personality just by looking at his brush work.

"Describe yourself through your work," I said.

"I like to write the words boldly," he answered. "My body is small but I want to make my world bold. In that spirit, I like to live and look forward to the future."

He said he works at night when it's quiet and he can concentrate. Once he starts, he doesn't stop even to answer the telephone. It takes him four hours to do the Sutra, Buddhist sacred writing, he said. Before he begins, he washes and purifies himself.

Koho said calligraphy is similar to the martial arts in that both are a means to seek the path. "What path?" I asked. "That is difficult to answer," he said.

He said he is happy in the seeking when he works at calligraphy. He feels a sense of unity. Sometimes he'll work for a month on one word before he's satisfied with it. For all his devotion to the art, he can't make a living at it. During the

day, he was working part time as a tour driver for Japanese visitors who had no idea he is an artist. He also teaches three classes in calligraphy to adults and during the school year to high schools in seven different schools.

Koho admitted that the market for calligraphy is not exactly booming. For his biggest commission he did the set used in the filming of *Karate Kid II* which starred Pat Morita and was filmed at Kuuloa on the island of Oahu.

Diet Pepsi With Mozart

Concert musicians may be born, not made, but practice makes them better. This is a truth well known to the patrons of Phillip's Lunch House on Kapiolani Boulevard, an establishment operated by a Korean immigrant family in a little corner off a parking lot. Customers get violin concertos performed live with their late afternoon snacks whether they like it or not. And most of them like it.

Carl Sanche from a health food store down the street sipped his Diet Pepsi at a front table while sixth-grader Khullip Jeung, son of the proprietor, stood under the breakfast menu on the wall and practiced his violin for a music lesson. The arpeggios of a concerto by Mozart soared among the booths as Khullip's mother sliced meat at the counter.

An older gentleman, reading the editorial page at another table, finally got up and left. But Sanche said he likes to hear Khullip practice on his violin.

So does Art Awai, vice president of an insurance company upstairs. "The boys practice quite a bit here," he admitted. "Especially on weekends. When the older boy is here, he corrects the younger one. I like to hear them practice."

Khullip's older brother is Phillip Jeung, now attending the University of Southern California on a full scholarship.

Khullip goes to the University of Hawaii Lab School. Both boys are straight–A students and both play the violin. Their favorite place to practice is the lunch house. When Phillip is home from USC, they fill even the parking lot with music.

"Khullip stays in here and Phillip goes outside," explained their father, Hyon-Jin Jeung, a Korean immigrant who taught sociology in high school at home. "The security guard came and said Phillip had to stop. I told him this is my place and he can practice when he wants to."

When you figure that both boys practice their violins up to three hours a day, the security guard may have a point. But their father takes the equally sensible view that the security guard should simply learn to like classical music. So Phillip's Lunch House may be the best friend the Honolulu Symphony ever had.

In fact, concertmaster Kathy Lucktenberg agreed to be Khullip's violin teacher. He has been playing since he was four years old in Korea and joined the Honolulu Youth Symphony when he was eight. A Women's Association for the Honolulu Symphony scholarship pays for his violin lessons, his father said.

When the celebrated concert violinist Cho Liang Lin performed in Honolulu, Khullip asked if he could try out Lin's priceless Stradivarius. The concert violinist said, "Yes." Khullip described this magic moment for the Hawaii Educational Association Essay Contest and won second place for grades four to six.

Hyon-Jin said he doesn't know which of his two sons is more talented. The oldest asked to play the oboe in the school band when he was in the second grade in Korea, but quickly switched to the violin. By the time he was ready for college in the United States, he was offered a full scholarship at the University of Mississippi. But he picked USC because it is closer to Hawaii, his father said.

Hyon-Jin brought his family to Honolulu in 1982. He has shipped on a fishing boat, worked in a shoe repair shop and held down a job as handyman in Hawaii Kai to keep his sons in violin lessons. He and his wife opened the diner in 1986. The family had to leave one rental apartment because the neighbors complained about so much violin practicing.

But Hyon-Jin is determined to give his sons as much opportunity as he can to develop their talent. As Khullip wrote in his prize-winning essay: "Hawaii is a paradise for young musicians. Some day Hawaii will be proud of me because I will be one of Hawaii's famous violinists."

Onward Christian Samurai

Architecture in Hawaii has a long and unique history. You are no doubt aware that the steep, rain-shedding roof of the humble grass house is perpetuated in the roof lines of classy mansions of millionaires today. The palm thatched sun shade extension under which fishermen once mended their nets had become the lanai, an absolute must for every suburban home in Honolulu.

But you may have missed one of the more exotic architectural innovations here, a Japanese feudal castle which is as Hawaiian, in its own way, as Iolani Palace, the Aloha Tower, the historic New England frame mission houses or Wo Fat's ornate chop suey emporium. The castle is formally known as the Makiki Christian Church and it is located on Pensacola Street. In 1990 it underwent repair to celebrate the 85th anniversary of the founding of the church. That's how it came to my attention.

The first aspect of this startling structure that demands explanation is how do you repair a Japanese castle in the age of mass production? The answer, it turns out, is, "with difficulty."

"We looked high and low for somebody to replace a termite-riddled dolphin," said Cal Tottori, an engineer retired from the state Department of Transportation. He's in charge of the repair committee. The gilded dolphin, a roof ornament, is the Japanese version of the Christian fish symbol. It is used in Japan in place of the sign of the cross. Cost of replacing the two dolphins on the roof of Makiki Christian Church was listed in the restoration budget at $75,000.

"They were going to create a ceramic dolphin for us at the University of Hawaii," said Tottori. "Somebody suggested, 'Try the Polynesian Cultural Center. They have wood carvers there.' But that fell through, too. Then we heard about Hisabaru Nose, who worked on temples and shrines for 14 years in Japan before he became a contractor in Honolulu. So far as I know, he's the only one here who does this kind of work."

While repairs to the castle went forward, I investigated how it came to be built in the first place. Here's what I learned:

In 1905 an amazing man named Takie Okumura, part saint and part samurai, founded the Makiki Christian Church at the corner of Kinau and Pensacola Streets. His church members were Japanese immigrants who worked as servants for rich haoles in Manoa. The congregation prospered and built a modest little structure on the intersection.

By the 1920s, Honolulu's churches had come up in the world. Central Union, the haole church, built its stately New England spire on Punahou Street. Then the Chinese Christian Church moved into the handsome building with a pagoda motif across from McKinley High School on King Street.

But it was not until 1932 that the Rev. Okumura revealed his dream to glorify the Lord with a church like none other in Honolulu. It would look like Kochi Castle in whose shadow he grew up on the island of Shikaku in faraway Japan. Church member Masayuki Tokioka, 93 when I talked to him,

remembers discussions in the congregation about this breathtaking idea.

Tokioka at the time was a recent graduate of the Harvard Business School. Even with diploma in hand, there were few openings for executive positions in Honolulu for the son of a Japanese immigrant nursery operator. But Tokioka had a secret weapon. He went to Sunday school at the Makiki Christian Church where a *haole* taught the Bible verses. This was the only haole in the church. It had been the Rev. Okumura's idea. Christ's teachings applied to all. This haole introduced Tokioka to the president of the International Trust Company which Tokioka eventually took over in the course of building a financial empire.

You see, young Tokioka had a lot of get-up-and-go. He had been a 112-pound fullback on the McKinley High School football team. He had also learned to surf at Waikiki, having purchased a redwood board bigger than himself in 1909 for one dollar from another fellow on the beach. Tokioka also taught his friend, Suyeki Okumura, son of the pastor, how to ride the waves. They were the only Japanese surfers on the beach dominated by Hawaiians and haoles. There was one Chinese. Tokioka is now the dean of Honolulu's financial community. Okumura, 79 when he recalled his surfing days, is a veteran corporate attorney.

Anyway, Tokioka remembered that fellow church members were not so sure they wanted a Japanese castle for a church. Maybe a European cathedral would be better. "I said, 'This is Hawaii, not Europe.'" he explained. "They said, 'Yes, this is Hawaii, not Japan. There are no castles in Hawaii.'" So we took a vote and the castle won. We all respected Okumura."

The board at the Hawaiian Evangelical Association was also a little nervous about the Okumura's castle. "Isn't the castle a symbol of war?" they asked.

"The castle in feudal Japan was a stronghold to maintain

peace and order," explained Okumura, a student of history. He pointed out that Hisahide Matsunaga, a Christian feudal lord, in 1560 built a five-story tower to worship the Lord of Heaven. A castle, therefore, was the first structure erected in Japan to glorify the Christian God. Dr. Theodore Richards, member of the board, agreed that it was better to preserve Japanese culture than to merely copy American ways.

The cost came to $75,000 and Okumura could find only one architect capable of drawing the blueprints for a Japanese Castle. Young Tokioka advised the committee to ask for financing from outside the church. "You talk nice but how much are you going to give?" said Okumura.

Tokioka said he had saved $400 to buy Christmas presents for his wife and three children. He went to them and said they would listen to the church bell instead of opening presents that year. He gave the whole $400 to build the castle.

The Island Way of Travel

Fear of Flying

Hawaii has always been a long way from anywhere. Since passenger ships have fallen on hard times, that means most visitors arrive and depart by air. Residents of the 50th State must fly across the sea to get from one island to another. Businessmen in Honolulu fly hundreds of thousands of miles a year to negotiate deals in boardrooms all the way from Tokyo to New York. In Hawaii, vacation trips to Las Vegas and Disneyland are popular. Students depart every fall for Mainland colleges. So you can understand how inconvenient it must be in Hawaii to be afraid to fly.

That is why the Fear of Flying Class offered at The Queen's Medical Center Health Clinic provides a welcome service. The director explained that the most common phobias in Honolulu are fear of driving and fear of flying. The six-week program is given in association with Hawaiian Air Lines and Pacific Anxiety Resources, an outfit which specializes in teaching people to cope with panic in elevators, tunnels, airplanes, downtown traffic, etc.

And that is why I found myself boarding a Hawaiian Airlines flight to Kauai one afternoon in December of 1988 with a group of very special passengers. They had just completed the Fear of Flying course and were about to try their new wings.

"I can't believe I'm doing this," said Stephenie Moderow as she fastened her seat belt. "I haven't flown in 22 years."

Dr. Edward Pontius, clinical director of the class, sat beside her as copilot. Other volunteers, graduates of previous classes, accompanied each student to give confidence.

Bob Ankersmit, a carpenter who hails from Washington State, said the last time he had boarded an airplane he got so scared that he made them open the door before takeoff and let him out. He hadn't flown since. "I came here three and a half years ago on a 40-foot sailboat, and I've been stuck on Oahu ever since because I was afraid to fly," he said.

Louise Souza said she always had to steel herself to fly to the Neighbor Islands for funerals and weddings. But it had been 20 years since she'd flown to the Mainland. "I'd make plans for a trip, but my feet just wouldn't get on the airplane," she said. Rose Nabarrete, an escrow officer, said she had to take Dramamine and then a drink to knock her out when she boarded an airplane because of the panic she felt in the air.

The doors closed. Jet engines started to whine. Flight attendants checked to make sure everybody had fastened their seat belts.

"I just can't believe I'm doing this," said Stephenie over and over. She sat very erect beside the window, next to Pontius, breathing deeply and trying to relax the way they taught her in class. Rose had brought along a small tape recorder. She immediately put on the earphones and turned on a tape made by clinical social worker Bill Watts giving instructions on how to relax, breathe deeply and control panic.

Also on the flight was Lauri Geier, a Hawaiian Airlines pilot, who conducted one of the ground classes. She had explained that turbulence in the air may be uncomfortable but not fatal, that wings don't fall off planes and that the bumps and knocks heard before takeoff are just baggage being unloaded, not a spy attaching a bomb to the fuselage. "It really helped a lot when the pilot explained about air waves," said Rose, "that the plane doesn't just fall. And about the noises you hear. That calms me down."

Stephenie remained erect in her seat during takeoff. Pontius told her the worse was over because getting on the plane was the hardest. Now she could sit back and wait for the end of the flight. It wasn't long before the students were chatting like regular passengers, not fugitives from a horror movie. By the time we got to Kauai, the tension level had come way down. In spite of a bumpy landing, everybody clapped.

Stephenie ran into the terminal to call her husband on Oahu. Louise ran in to tell her father who lives on Kauai. The flight back was easier still, like a party, with everybody confidently chatting instead of trying to breathe deep. "That first five minutes out of Honolulu was pretty scary," Bob Ankersmit confessed. "But my partner got me breathing. By the time we leveled off, it was a piece of cake. I looked out of the window and all that stuff."

Both Rose and Louise had already made plans to fly to the Mainland over the holidays for family reunions. Both said they think they'll make it this time. "I feel 20 pounds lighter," said Stephenie. "I feel so FREE."

Airport Sign Language

We all know that airports, once they are put into operation, somehow never get finished. They grow like topsy, expanding here and there, sending out new tunnels like roots of a tree, putting in extra shops and security posts and generally making it more and more confusing for travelers. Honolulu International Airport, for example, is the biggest construction project in Hawaii. It's been under construction since the Wall Street panic of 1929, at least.

That's why Warland Kealoha is probably our most indispensable public servant. You may wish to offer a prayer of thanks to him the next time you pass through one of the terminals because Kealoha is the person who makes the signs

that tell you which way to turn in the largest, most confused complex of buildings in the state of Hawaii. Without him, nobody would be able to get to Maui, much less Australia. If he went on strike, going to the bathroom at the airport would become impossible.

"I remember them adding onto it ever since I was young," he said. And each time somebody digs up a sidewalk or puts up another barricade, Kealoha has to make more signs. "Do you ever get caught up?" I asked him. "No, no. Sometimes I fall a week behind," answered Honolulu's busiest sign maker.

At the moment he was working on baggage claim signs because the Ewa (west) side of the baggage claim area had been shut down and everybody had to detour to the Diamond Head side (east). To keep people from breaking their necks over a distance the length of a football field required five or more BAGGAGE CLAIM signs with arrows pointing in the right direction. Meanwhile, Air New Zealand complained that its sign was missing and they would like to know when it would be replaced.

You can imagine what it was like before the Department of Transportation, Airports Division, got a sign-making computer to speed things up. Now Kealoha can whip up a REST ROOM sign with an arrow pointed in the right direction in ten to fifteen minutes. Before, people jumped from one foot to another while a maintenance person hand-lettered the sign. It could take all day, said Kealoha.

Even with the computer, keeping up with progress is a challenge. Say construction workers dig up the sidewalk in front where people get out of their cars and taxis. The first thing that happens is that passengers get lost. "Where's American?" they ask. "It was here the last time." This means the porters must explain over and over again that you have to walk AROUND the dug-up sidewalk and that the shuttle bus stop has been moved temporarily.

The mission of Kealoha and his handy dandy sign-making computer is to avoid all this confusion. But it's very difficult because the airport is a complicated city within a city with its own bureaucracy. Tearing up the sidewalk and making the necessary signs requires the cooperation of the contractor doing the work, of the Transportation Department engineer in charge, of the Visitor Information Center, and of the airport manager and the operations manager who send memos to the airlines whose signs have to be moved.

Do you have any idea how many signs it takes in the airport just to get you on a plane for Tokyo? I'll tell you. 1. Airline sign outside. 2. Agricultural inspection sign. 3. Ticket counter sign. 4. Roughly eight signs to the gate. 5. Three signs to get you through security checks. 6. Two signs to the coffee shop if you're hungry. 7. Two signs to Duty Free Shoppers if you want to buy a bottle of booze. 8. Three signs at least to get you to a rest room. 9. A Customs Area sign. 10. Three or more NO SMOKING signs.

That's 25 signs. And you can enlarge that number by any multiple you wish because any portion of the two miles of corridors in the terminals can be changed at any time. "I like to watch people follow my signs," Kealoha said. "Even people who live here and think they know where to go get lost because that door isn't there anymore."

How To Travel In New Shoes

Long distance travelers from Hawaii have to grapple with problems that probably don't seem important to people anywhere else. But for us they require serious consideration. For example, every fall *kamaaina* residents find themselves once again on the horns of an annual dilemma – what to wear on a trip to the Mainland. What is the alternative to sandals in chilly St. Paul? How do you survive a blizzard in Boston when you don't own an overcoat? Where can you borrow a sweater to wear in Maine?

Every now and then I consult local experts about how to cope with these predicaments. The last time I took such a survey was about eight years ago but the advice is just as good now as ever. Are you ready? First we will consider shoes.

"I think it's more of a problem for women than men," said Marilyn Hillendahl, wife of a former Bankoh economist. "Most of us who have lived here a long time wear sandals because they're so comfortable. When I wear pumps on a trip to the Mainland, I get blisters." You have to agree with her that getting blisters while hiking in Manhattan is no fun. "I immediately take my shoes right off when I arrive in a hotel lobby," she added. "You can always spot a woman from Hawaii waiting to register because she's barefoot." Other women use Band-Aids to cushion the blisters.

Donna Bauman, wife of the general manager of Coca-Cola in Hawaii at the time, said she refuses to spend a lot of money on shoes that will just sit in the closet when she gets back from a trip. "We just returned from Alaska and Wisconsin," she said. "Before we left, I bought a good-looking pair of dressy hush puppy loafers here in Kailua for $1 at a garage sale. In New Zealand, I wore my tennis shoes to a formal dinner one night under a long dress. Nobody noticed."

Marjorie Guy, owner of Four Seasons Travel Agency, recommends that women who buy new pumps for a Main-land trip wear them around the house for a week. "A lot of women who buy new shoes take them off on the airplane," explained Guy. "Then their feet swell and they can't get them on again." Guy has typed up a set of calisthenics you can do in your seat to get your feet back to normal. One woman whose feet swell is Jean Smith, wife of a past president of the

American Consulting Engineers Council. "I bring along canvas shoes with rope soles to wear on the airplane," she said.

So much for blisters and swollen feet. Another common problem of both male and female *kamaainas* is how to keep warm in sub-zero temperatures. The definitive answer is BORROWING.

"The greatest discovery I ever made was long johns a friend loaned me at Lake Tahoe," said Jean Smith. "They're the meshy type with a scoop neck. You can even wear them with a long dress in the evening." The wife of a retired Pan American World Airways maintenance superintendent said he bought a pair of long johns while attending a training school in London and they've been traveling in suitcases of friends ever since.

Bill Bauman said he loans out a Humphrey Bogart trench coat which goes all over the world. There was a camel-hair coat for female travelers on loan at the Assistance League of Hawaii thrift shop. It's probably worn out by now. Bank of Hawaii used to have a felt hat and an overcoat hanging in the hall for any employee who had to make a quick trip to the Mainland. But that valuable service has been discontinued. Guy said she keeps a tuxedo in the closet on loan for good customers. All local travelers recommend thrift shops as good places to buy warm clothes at reasonable prices.

I used to have what must have been the most-borrowed overcoat in Hawaii. I bought it in 1948 when I was a junior at the University of Minnesota. The overcoat hung in the closet between trips by friends to places like Butte, Montana and Madison, Wisconsin. It finally fell apart. Then I found a stylish, World War II Navy officer's greatcoat with gold buttons at the close out sale of a theatrical costume supply. You're welcome to borrow it if you're willing to pass for a war hero.

How to Accommodate to Taste

Years of accommodation to the likes and dislikes of visitors to our shores have trained us to be adaptable. When tourists required assistance to learn how to surf and paddle outrigger canoes, we invented beach boys. Because travelers from Ohio never seemed to care much for fish and poi, we added native delicacies like chicken and roast beef to commercial luaus. In recent years, inspired by a flood of visitors from Japan, we have created a whole new array of Hawaiian traditions like formal, Western style weddings in tuxedos and bridal gowns at the church of one's choice with a picture of the bride and groom included in the package.

Another startling example of our ability to accommodate to Japanese visitors is an entirely fresh look at native Hawaiian food. We are not referring to macadamia nut ice cream, nor guava sherbet, nor Dole pineapple juice, nor even fresh caught mahimahi. We're talking steak and lobster here.

When I first heard of this development, I didn't believe it. So I spent a few hours at one of our foremost restaurants, Nicholas Nickolas, where Yoko and Naoki Mitooka of Kobe, Japan, a honeymoon couple, had come to sample Hawaii's tropical atmosphere and to taste the foods of the natives. Sure enough, they ordered steak and lobster. So did every other Japanese couple in the place including Mr. and Mrs. Shoji Susaki of Kanagawa Prefecture. The Susakis had eaten pineapple only once during their Hawaiian vacation and that was from a fruit bowl sitting in their hotel room on arrival.

The traditional foods these visitors have come to associate with Hawaii are steak and lobster. They had never heard of *saimin* and Mrs. Susaki said she doesn't like the rice in Hawaii because it's sticky "like glue" although the rice in Guam isn't too bad. Satisfying these preferences of the Japanese palate has become big business in Honolulu. One authority on the subject is Tina Marie Machado Plakourakis who had gone into the restaurant tour business for Japanese visitors.

"They love their steak and lobster," Tina Marie said. "We've offered them veal and fish but they don't want fish. They can eat that at home. When they come to Hawaii they expect steak and lobster."

Naoki, who's a dentist in Kobe, explained why Japanese have come to regard steak and lobster as Hawaii's most desirable native food, even though most of it doesn't come from here. It's shipped in frozen. "My dinners tonight cost $60," he said through an interpreter. "In Kobe, it would cost at least twice that much." So Japanese guide books on Hawaii always recommend steak and lobster. Neither he nor Yoko had ever heard of *saimin*. They'd had *sashimi* (raw fish) only once during their stay. The Susakis hadn't had sashimi at all.

"Japanese visitors don't eat Japanese foods while they're in Hawaii," Tina Marie said. "Their favorite soup is clam chowder. For an appetizer, they order shrimp cocktail with the cocktail sauce. For dessert, we've tried cheesecake, chocolate mousse and crepes. They prefer rainbow sherbet."

Frankly, I was dismayed to discover that our Japanese visitors had been deprived of saimin, Hawaii's favorite noodle soup, all these years so I invited Yoko and Naoki to have a bowl with me the next day. They were staying at the Hyatt Regency in Waikiki. Before that, they were at the Kapalua Resort on Maui, both definitely high class hotels. We drove in my Volkswagen to a saimin stand in Moiliili, where Kazuko Sinoto joined us. She is the author of a book on Japanese immigrants to Hawaii. Her husband was chairman of anthropology at the Bishop Museum.

I was somewhat concerned that a saimin stand in Moiliili might not be up to the standard expected by the charming Mitookas. But they liked it. Naoki complained that tours never took him to relaxing restaurants like saimin stands where he didn't have to wear a coat. He and Yoko gobbled their saimin with gusto while Kazuko told them about its origin and I took notes because she's an authority.

She said advertisements in Honolulu's old Japanese language newspaper, the *Yamato Shimbun*, predecessor of the *Japan Times*, listed Japanese noodle shops as far back as 1896. Jack Tasaka, retired reporter and radio announcer, told her that Japanese businessmen back then considered Chinese noodles more exotic than their own. But noodles in a Chinese restaurant were expensive. Cut rate Chinese noodles in Japanese noodle shops, therefore, sold well. They called the dish saimin. At least, this is one theory about its origin. The noodles were served at the beginning from mobile lunch wagons. Pat Bacon at the Bishop Museum said she can remember permanent saimin stands as far back as 1928.

Anyway, Yoko and Naoki had a marvelous time eating saimin and insisted we all have our picture taken with their camera by a passerby outside the saimin stand. I have a hunch other Japanese visitors would like saimin, too, if they only knew about it. Our bowls cost $2.60 apiece and it was all we could eat.

Around Oahu In Six Years

A common complaint about islands is their small size. You can't jump in the car and drive for a thousand miles in any direction. After 130 miles you start going around Oahu again. The Big Island of Hawaii is 300 miles around but even that is not enough for people who haven't learned the island way of travel. That is, don't worry about getting there. Enjoy yourself along the way.

Harmony Bentosino, wife of a Honolulu police officer, learned the secret all by herself. She said she bought a book in March of 1987 about the beaches of Oahu. Since she worked mostly at night, she had days free so she decided to visit each of the beaches in the book. It was so much fun that she decided to go back and explore the shoreline between the beaches. That's how she began working her way on foot around the island of Oahu. I didn't hear about this epic journey until she'd been at it for almost two years.

By that time she was exploring the Pearlridge Shopping Center. "I kinda got addicted to the movie theaters there," she confessed. "I've seen two double features besides shopping. Another place I liked is Magic Island. I spent three days there reading."

At the rate Harmony is going, she will make "Around The World In Eighty Days" seem like a speed record. Her movie will be entitled, "Around Oahu in Six Years," and it could revolutionize the travel industry. She spends practically nothing and doesn't even have to pack. "I just go on days when I have time," she explained. "I start where I left off before. I love traveling this way and I can travel without leaving my husband and cats. It's so convenient."

Harmony said the only thing that may interrupt her grand tour is having a baby. She and her policeman husband were married about the time the journey began and she's afraid it might take too long to finish before starting a family. Harmony doesn't take roads unless it is absolutely necessary. She walks along the shoreline. This sometimes leads to problems. At Koko Marina she was attacked by a dog and had to jump into the water and swim for safety. Blocked by cliffs beyond Hanauma Bay, she climbed over the summit of Koko Head. She swam part of the way around Wailupe Peninsula.

She said she wears a swimming suit under a pair of shorts and a T-shirt with a fanny pack to carry a sandwich, soda, some money or whatever. "I try to do everything there is to do along the way," she said. "That's why it is taking me so long. I've walked the rims of Koko Head and Diamond Head

craters, gone para-sailing at Waikiki and visited the zoo and aquarium. When I get to an interesting restaurant I stop. I had to pass up John Dominis but went back later with my husband when we were dressed up."

Harmony said her most exciting adventures was walking around the reef runway at Honolulu Airport after a guard outside the fence told her she could. From there she walked around Hickam Air Force Base and the shore of Pearl Harbor, something probably no civilian has ever done before. "Nobody stopped me," she said. "When I got lost and asked to find the Arizona Memorial, a security guard pointed the way."

She said she may be able to go faster now that she's passed metropolitan Honolulu but she doesn't care how long it takes. "Before, I always wanted to live on another island," she said. "This trip has made me appreciate Oahu. To me, a circle symbolizes wholeness and unity, completeness. I feel that if I circle the island, it will become part of me."

Fabio, the Fearless Florentine

The communications barrier has always been a problem for travelers in foreign countries. Fortunately for U.S. citizens, English is the most widely spoken language in the world. It's the form of communication in Waikiki, of course, with Japanese next. Germans, Frenchmen, Russians, Spanish, Chinese and other citizens of the globe get along as best they can. Silvestri Fabio of Italy was another matter entirely.

It wasn't that Italian is such an exotic language in Hawaii. There are quite a few Italians here. But Fabio didn't speak Italian. He didn't speak at all. He didn't hear, either.

He turned up one midnight at the front desk of the Outrigger Reef Tower Hotel with a reservation slip at the height of the tourist season. How he ever got from the airport to Waikiki is a mystery because Fabio was never able to explain it. But there he was at midnight unable to say or hear a word. An assistant manager checked him in and gave him a key to one of the 38,000 rooms in Waikiki.

The next morning Fabio went to a travel desk in the busy hotel lobby. He wrote "Italiano" on a piece of paper and handed it to Stewart White, the travel agent. Then Fabio waved his arms a lot. White found himself at a complete loss. Nothing he said registered with his new client. He had absolutely no idea how to respond. "We couldn't communicate," he said later.

About that time, White's wife, Margaret, who was born with cerebral palsy, dropped by to see her husband. She said she understood immediately that the mysterious stranger was unable to speak or hear as a result of the same disease that had almost crippled her. Margaret White immediately became a one-woman reception committee on call eight hours a day, seven days a week.

With an Italian dictionary, she was able to make a little contact. Also, the man wrote his name, Fabio. Then Margaret found an Italian-speaking man who took Fabio home for an Italian dinner. Another clue emerged. They played chess and Fabio absolutely wiped out his host who considered himself a good chess player. How had a person who couldn't speak or hear learned to play championship chess? What was he doing in Hawaii? How did he get here?

Fabio was featured on a TV news broadcast and invitations rolled in for a *luau*, a night club show and a circle-island tour. The mysterious Italian had a wonderful time. But who was he? Where did he live in Italy? Was his family concerned about him? How had he earned enough money to take a trip to Hawaii?

The pieces finally fell into place when Shirley BeNard, a professional sign language interpreter, volunteered to help.

Both her parents are deaf. She can sign not only the alphabet, but in pantomime, the universal language used by American Indians. She consented to interpret for an interview with Fabio so that we could all find out what in the world brought him to Hawaii.

It was an amazing interview. Shirley doesn't speak Italian. Fabio doesn't know English. Yet they understood each other, arms and hands and fingers flying as his story unfolded.

He explained, looking up words in the dictionary when gestures failed, that he is from Florence, was 27 at the time, one of two brothers. "My mother and father don't care about me," he gestured. "So what? I don't care. My grandmother took me in when I was a baby. I grew. I grew. She took care of me. I wouldn't say, 'so what,' to her. No, never. My grandmother let me be free."

In pantomime, Fabio told about his painful struggle to learn to walk by supporting himself on parallel bars. He placed chairs in two rows and walked between, supporting himself with his arms. Shirley spoke the words he said in gestures, "When I was small, I couldn't walk. So what if I couldn't walk? I learned slow, slow. A little at a time. Every day, seven days a week."

He said he had been working for the past three years as a mail sorter in an insurance company, putting money away in the bank until he had enough for vacations. Before, he visited France and Germany with a friend. This time he went alone.

Why Hawaii? "I thought, I thought about it. I'm in Italy now. Same old place. So, phooey. I want to go to Hawaii."

What did his fellow workers think about his trip? "They were surprised. Their jaws dropped when I went."

How does he like Waikiki Beach? "I like to swim. I do it all the time. In Italy, the beach is stinky. Here the beach is perfect. Kiss, kiss (in gestures). It is out of sight."

Margaret White said she understands very well Fabio's fierce determination to demonstrate his independence by coming alone to Hawaii. She said doctors told her mother when she was born that she would never function normally. But her mother did not give up. She encouraged Margaret to be self-sufficient. Her victory is that she was able to marry and keep house for her husband.

"It's got to be the most frustrating thing in the world to have a mind like Fabio's and not be able to talk to people," she said.

Horsing Around Before Marriage

One of the souvenirs on sale in the sidewalk shops along Kalakaua Avenue in Waikiki is a economy-priced garment with lettering on the back, "My Parents Went To Hawaii And All They Brought Me Was This Damn T-shirt." Actually, visitors to the Islands bring back all sorts of things including lava rock, sunburns, overdrawn credit cards and a knowledge of how to mispronounce numerous Hawaiian street names. Evelyn Skinner of Squeeze Bottom, Tennessee brought back stars in her eyes.

Evelyn, at age 60, was in love as the result of a fairy tale romance which followed some horsing around with Bob Ross, a bachelor aged 58. He was, if that's possible, more in love than Evelyn.

It all began when Evelyn came to Hawaii with her father and stepmother. They checked into the high rise Hilton Hawaiian Village and sat on their lanai to admire the coconut palms. Every day a horse-drawn carriage clip-clopped by on the street below. In the driver's seat sat a handsome gentleman in a top had and tuxedo. After a week, Evelyn suggested to her parents that they go for a ride. The driver was, you guessed it, Bob Ross.

She said later she still can't believe what happened. "The first thing the driver said to me was, 'Would you like to go for a cruise, go out to dinner or get married?' Well, it was just foolishness so I said, 'I'd rather get married.'"

Bob said, for him, it was love at first sight. "The moment I spotted her beautiful brown eyes, I knew that this was it," he said. "She's got a great figure, too. I waited 18 years for a woman like her. I've prayed to the Lord for it and He finally sent me an angel."

He said his first wife died at age 35. Evelyn had also been married and now has children and grandchildren. Bob said neither of them felt over 30 when they met.

"The very first day he bought me a friendship ring," said Evelyn. "He wanted my picture. The next day he read me some of his poetry. The day after he took me to breakfast and then to a park. When we got back to the hotel, he asked my father, 'What would you say if I told you I wanted to marry your daughter?' My father said, 'Well, she's 60 years old, she ought to be able to make up her own mind.'"

Evelyn's mind was already made up. Even after she got back to Squeeze Bottom, she said, "It's like a fairy tale. I'm still pinching myself to make sure it's true. We talk on the phone at least twice a day."

Bob said the phone bill became astronomical but he didn't care. "It's worth every penny. I never thought I'd fall in love again but I did. There are not too many good women around these days. She's a Christian lady and I'm a Christian man. I look for somebody who is sincere and she's that."

He said he drove a horse and carriage for 20 years in New York before coming to Waikiki. While Evelyn went back to Squeeze Bottom to arrange her affairs, he moved into a bigger apartment and bought three matching aloha shirt and muumuu outfits. They were married under a tropical tree on Waikiki Beach and, at this writing, have lived happily ever after.

Evolution of the Good Life

Keeping Up With Who We Are

By this time it must be clear to everyone who has been patient enough to read this far that Hawaii is a complicated, multi-dimensional place unlike anywhere else on earth. Yet, it is important to understand that nothing stays the same. That's why this book is not an exercise in nostalgia but simply a report of who we are today. In ten years we will be something else, recognizable but different because we are constantly evolving. This is not something to be discouraged about but, rather, to welcome. Life would soon get boring otherwise.

One handy reference for keeping up with who we are today is the telephone book, a useful social document that accurately records the changes in our tastes and interests and relationships every year. For example, from the telephone book we learn that the leading family of Oahu is not Dillingham nor Baldwin nor any of the names most often seen in the gossip columns. The leading family of Honolulu is Lee because there are more Lees listed in the phone book than any other, Lee being Chinese as well as Korean and Caucasian.

Traditionally, the Wong numbers come in second. Then come the Youngs. The Changs and the Chuns for years waged a fierce, see-saw battle for fourth and fifth place until 1977 when the Smiths overtook the Chuns, a startling development, putting the Smiths in fifth place and dropping the Chuns to sixth. The Nakamuras came next, then the Lums followed by the Yamamotos. In the same year, the Browns almost made the top ten for the first time with the Millers and Williamses in close contention. Obviously a population shift was in progress as immigration from the east exceeded that from the west. Ten years later a new flow from Southeast Asia seems to have reversed the process once more.

The Yellow Pages are just as revealing. Listings under chop suey restaurants have always made Chinese chow

Honolulu's favorite, that is, until fast foods hit our island. In 1977, pizza jumped from two pages to four and one-half pages an, unprecedented, history-making shift in taste because there were only three and one-fourth pages of chop suey that year. But pizza proved to be a fad, a flash in the pan, a mere passing fancy. The last edition of the Yellow Pages showed chop suey once more in firm control.

An even more significant social change is in progress. Automobiles, as reflected in number of Yellow Pages devoted to their sales, spare parts, tires, mufflers, etc., have been our dominant and abiding love. Down through the years, we have placed more advertisements out of concern for our automobiles than any other aspect of our lives. Concern for our health has always followed as reflected in the number of pages devoted to physicians. Television, of course, made a spectacular rise at one time but has never threatened to replace autos or doctors. The same for computers. Carpets, roofing and plumbing have always been dear to our hearts but not like the automobile. Schools and churches are usually near the bottom of the list.

As I remember when I began reviewing the phone book in the 1960s, attorneys ranked down around with plumbers. However, in the 1980s the residents of Honolulu seemed to take a new interest in suing each other. In 1985, attorneys leapfrogged into second place with 29 pages of listings in the Yellow Pages, up from nine pages in 1978. By 1987, attorneys filled 43 pages. This rose dramatically to 66 pages in 1988 while physicians listed only 48 pages, putting attorneys for the first time within shouting distance of automobiles.

It was no wonder. The Yellow Pages devoted to attorneys had become the most exciting in the book. Merely by letting our fingers do the walking we could sue for personal injury, workers' compensation, failure analysis, construction defects, sales purchases, toxicology, computer fraud, divorce, taxes, wrongful discharge (getting fired), civil rights, employment discrimination, auto defects, medical malpractice, accidental death, insurance claims, aviation and maritime accidents, toxic and chemical exposure, traffic violations, drug offenses, breach of contract, drunken driving, asbestos claims, brain injury, motorcycle accidents, bankruptcy and credit harassment.

Our enthusiasm for suing each other in 1989 brought lawyers to within three pages of automobiles, 77 to 80. And as we moved into the 1990s, the impossible happened. For the first time in history, attorneys became kings of the Yellow Pages. They surged to 79 pages filled with a breathtaking assortment of litigation, compared to only 71 pages for brake linings, body and fender work, spare parts and tune-ups.

It is a statistic that boggles the mind. It is as if Martha Washington were to admit that she had at last lost interest in George. On the other hand, the trend may reverse itself. Who knows, we may get tired of suing each other and take up weight lifting. The Yellow Pages are as unpredictable as the stock market because they reflect us. Before that happens, we will sketch a few more scenes in this last chapter about the good life as we live it today. Enjoy them while you can.

Whatever Happened to Discoverers' Day?

One secret of how to enjoy the good life is not to always grumble about changes, although they will probably turn out bad, but to think about how pleasantly surprised you'd be if things turned out right for once. And they do. You don't always have to grit your teeth when you smile. The aloha spirit provides abundant opportunities for unalloyed enjoyment of life. A lot more, in fact, than if you grumble all the time.

That is why we are enjoying our new holiday, Martin Luther King Day, initiated here in 1989. For many years we have looked up to Dr. King as a inspiration. He represents humility and decency and courage in the face of prejudice and narrow-minded disapproval. Meanwhile we are keeping our fingers crossed that something doesn't happen to spoil it. This is because we didn't have very good luck with the holiday for which we traded it, Discoverers' Day.

Sometimes things just don't work out. You have to admit it was a good idea. Maybe it was Christopher Columbus who got us off on the wrong foot. For better than half a century the rest of the nation tried to get us interested in Columbus Day on October 12. It was like forcing somebody from Brooklyn to eat *poi*. Mainlanders celebrated Columbus Day with parades and high-flown speeches from Fresno to Atlantic City. Not in Hawaii. We went about our business as usual. The governor didn't even issue a proclamation. Finally, in 1962, the Knights of Columbus started an annual Columbus Day dinner. But their hearts weren't in it.

It seemed as though we did more arguing than celebrating. If you asked an Irishman who discovered America, he'd say, "St. Brendan, 900 years before that upstart Italian." Norwegians were equally convinced that Leif Erikson discovered America about 1000 A.D. while Chinese scholars insisted that it was a fellow named Hui Shen who sailed to Mexico in 452 A.D. and returned to China in 499 A.D. The truth is, the Indians were already there.

"There is a good deal of unreality and stage business in the discovery game which, after all, consists in finding out what plenty of people already knew," wrote a Dr. W. W. Slaten in 1934 after studying up on the subject. Slaten asked why we should credit Columbus with the discovery of America at all since it was a sailor named Rodrigo de Triana in the crow's nest who saw it first and yelled, "Land ho!"

This state of affairs continued in Hawaii until 1970 when an editor who works for a competing newspaper whose name we will not mention suggested that we have plenty of discoverers of our own right here at home. Why not celebrate ancient Hawaiian voyagers, Captain Cook and other Pacific explorers instead of Columbus? Everybody fell all over themselves endorsing the idea. In 1971 the Legislature passed a bill and Governor John Burns signed it into law. Discoverer's Day had come to Hawaii.

It turned out to be even more complicated than the hoorah about Columbus. You and I know who discovered Hawaii. But what about the dingaling across the street? Tour drivers on Kauai credit the menehune. There is still a faithful clique promoting Hawaii Loa. Strong support continues for a lost tribe of Israel.

Captain Cook has as many competitors as the early Hawaiians. After all, Spanish galleons were sailing across the Pacific before Cook was born. Robert Langdon of Australia wrote a whole book, *The Lost Caravel*, about it. And as far back as 1899 one John W. Stanley wrote that it was a Spanish navigator, Gaetano, who discovered Hawaii in 1542, not James Cook in 1778. Local Portuguese have always disputed such Spanish pretension because they claim Gaetano as one of their own.

Maybe that's why Discoverers' Day never really got off the ground. Too many people were trying to take credit while the folks who discovered things were too busy to file a claim. I hope we don't make the same mistake about Martin Luther King Day. It doesn't matter who represents racial tolerance so long as we share the dream.

Cardboard Jones

In line with our goal of reporting some of the more subtle and impermanent expressions of aloha in this chapter, let me introduce to you Cardboard Jones who has never read Emerson's essays, cannot discuss with you the philosophy of Plato, but who has developed his own system to keep society from disintegrating into chaos. He gives tired shoppers at Ala Moana Center pieces of cardboard to sit on so their *okoles*, or backsides, won't get sore.

Every morning at 7 A.M. he arrives at the center with a red shopping bag full of squares of cardboard borrowed from the manager at Longs Drugs. Jones takes his station at the low concrete wall on the mall level along the Waikiki side of Sears facing Longs. This wall is covered with a pebbly surface that bites into the *okole*. When somebody sits on the wall, Jones shuffles over and politely hands him or her a piece of cardboard to sit on.

"It's a little shocking at first," admitted a shopper. "He doesn't say anything, just hands you the cardboard. Tourists, locals, everybody gets one."

About twenty old-timers make the wall their clubhouse. Albert Bishop has been coming for 18 years. K.P. Lee, who's about 90, still puts in an appearance now and then. But Cardboard Jones is the only one who gives out cardboard. For him it is a mission, a calling. His friends do yard work. Or chew the fat. Or play softball to pass the time. He gives out cardboard 12 hours a day, seven days a week.

"I like to make everybody happy," he explained. "There is a lady who comes every day and gives me two kisses. Just now a couple came by and said, 'We have been gone three years and you're still here. I think you're going to live to be a hundred.' Wives consult Cardboard Jones about their husbands. Husbands and wives agree to meet at Cardboard

Jones' after shopping. His fans recognize him when he dines at McDonald's.

Jones admits that he didn't think up the idea of cardboard sitting. It was a retired cab driver named Sam Ching who did it first about 20 years ago. But the two men have entirely different philosophies. "I didn't want to get my pants dirty when I sat down," said Ching, a dapper 81 at the time he was interviewed. "After all, I'm retired and I can't afford to get my pants washed more than every two or three weeks. Besides, the cement is cold and hard. So I got some cardboard to sit on."

Jones took this self-centered concept and turned it into a public utility. To him, everybody should be able to sit on cardboard, not just people with fancy pants. It's a matter of social justice. In fact, the manager of Sears gave Cardboard Jones a big scrap of carpet for extra luxurious sitting. Jones cut the carpet into twenty pieces. They are super comfortable on the *okole*. "But the carpet is heavy," he sighed. "I bring only eight pieces at a time to the shopping center."

Cardboard Jones said he lives alone, since his wife died, at the Central YMCA across the street from the shopping center. He generally has breakfast at Woolworth and dinner at Zippy's. He sometimes spends Christmas Eve at McDonald's in Waikiki. "Aren't you lonely?" I asked him. "No, he said. "Five ladies want me for companionship. I tell them I'm too busy. I've got a job to do."

Concertmaster of the Conch Shell

Every new generation in Hawaii produces its own musical stars. In the 1950s and 1960s, middle-aged ladies from Nebraska swooned to the soothing baritone of Alfred Apaka.

He was followed by the legendary Don Ho who makes the same audience swoon with *I'll Remember You*. Then came a new sound, still in vogue, invented by the Brothers Cazimero who mix a little humor and ancient Hawaii with their new sound. Before his memory passes from the scene, as it must eventually, let us pay homage also to Richard "Babe" Bell.

What Jascha Heifetz was to the violin, what Ignacy Paderewski was to the piano, what Louis Armstrong was to the trumpet, Babe Bell is to the conch shell. The soulful, dulcet tones of his conch shell heralded the inauguration of Governor John Waihee. Babe tooted for the General Motors Convention at the Sheraton-Waikiki Resort. He opened the First Federal Savings & Loan and has marched in both the Kamehameha Day and Aloha Week parades. To engage the artistic services of Babe and his conch shell, expect to pay at least $100 an hour. "That's if I have to open and close the program," he explained. "If I just blow the conch and go right home, it's only $75."

Every day at sunset, Babe lifts the conch shell to his lips in the outdoor lobby of the Ilikai Hotel and lets loose a moaning blast while his son-in-law and his daughter's boyfriend trot around the fountain and light the torches. "I've probably been blowing the conch shell longer any anybody in the world," Babe admitted modestly. "Before I came to the Ilikai, I blew the conch shell for luaus at the Royal Hawaiian Hotel."

Unlike most musical prodigies, Babe discovered his talent by accident. "It was about 1957," he said. "My wife was dancing the hula at the Royal Hawaiian for Haunanai Kahalewai. Boyfriends and husbands used to wait around for the women in the show to finish. So Haunanai said, 'I'm going to put you to work. You and you carry spears. You blow the conch shell.' Well, she's the boss so I got to learn.

"At first it was embarrassing, more air than sound. But I got pretty good at it. When I was in the ninth grade, I played trumpet in the band and you blow a conch shell like a trumpet. But you don't have a mouthpiece, just a hole to blow into. To make the sound, you have to vibrate the lips. The real trick first is to get a good conch shell. If you get one that's too big, it's like a tuba. Just blaaaaaah. It takes too much air. If you get one that's too small, it sounds tinny.

"I've got six conch shells at home; big ones, small ones. The one I use is medium size. A good conch shell in Hawaii costs $60 to $70. The best place to buy them is at Disneyland in L.A. They sell real good conch shells for $30. I was surprised."

Since the demand for conch shell blowers is not overwhelming, Babe makes his living during the day at the Gas Company. When he finishes work, he hurries to Iolani School to coach an outrigger canoe club. Then, at sunset, he drives to the Ilikai, changes into his red lava lava and Kamehameha cape, and blows the conch shell for the torch lighting ceremony. "I do it seven days a week," he said. "It doesn't matter where I am at sunset, I have to leave and go to the Ilikai. Sometimes I'm just starting the first course of a Chinese dinner. If I hurry, I can get back for the fourth course.

For all his stage experience, Babe is not used to the limelight. Being interviewed by *The Advertiser*, he said, made him nervous. That evening, the ancient Hawaiian torches placed around the outdoor lobby would not light. "I got so excited during the interview, I forgot to turn on the gas," he explained.

The Best *Kulolo* in the Clergy

Like musicians, artists and famous football stars, noted pastors at Kawaiahao Church also come and go. Kawaiahao Church is the Westminster Abbey of Honolulu. It was built a century and a half ago of coral block mined from the reef outside Honolulu Harbor. On the walls hang portraits of the distinguished ministers of the gospel who have preached in its koa pulpit to kings, presidents, generals and millionaires as well as common, ordinary Hawaiians who also make up the congregation.

The Rev. Hiram Bingham, leader of the first group of missionaries who arrived in Hawaii in 1820, founded this church and delivered fire and brimstone sermons to his followers. In recent times, the beloved Rev. Abraham Akaka became famous for sermons he preached with the aid of his ukulele. Retired now, he was also a champion surfer. His successor, the Rev. William Kaina, has found another way to bring followers into the fold.

Kahu Kaina (*kahu* is the Hawaiian term for pastor) is the champion *kulolo* maker of the Congregational Church in Hawaii. "He's the best," said one of his admiring congregation members. "He makes the best *kulolo* in Kawaiahao Church and all the other churches. When he makes, everybody wants to buy." This is important because *kulolo* is a favorite ingredient of a *luau* and benefit *luaus* or Hawaiian feasts are primary money makers for churches. Having a champion kulolo maker in the congregation is a real asset. To the uninitiated, kulolo is a chewy, sweet dessert with the consistency of plumb pudding. Kulolo is to a luau what baked Alaska is to a banquet in the posh Mauna Lani Resort on Hawaii.

The reason for *Kahu* Kaina's expertise in kulolo is because he comes from Kalapana on the Big Island which, as everybody knows, is the kulolo capital of Hawaii. "I started helping my parents make kulolo when I was eight years old," said the *kahu* as he stirred a pink mud puddle in a washtub with a wooden paddle. "Kalapana is noted for its kulolo. It's because of the coconuts and the honey. When Kalapana people make kulolo for a church benefit, it is sold before it's finished."

It was soon after Kaina became pastor at Kawaiahao Church that congregation members in charge of the *Kamehameha Day* luau woke up to what a gold mine they had in the pulpit. With the new kahu's kulolo on the menu, the luau couldn't miss. At the same time, the kahu wanted to teach the younger generation finer points of Hawaiiana like how much Karo syrup to put in with the brown sugar and honey. So both young and old come to assist in the kulolo making.

"We pulled four 80-pound bags of *taro* at Hanalei for the kulolo," said Tommy Kaneakua, luau chairman a year or two ago. "And we brought back 160 coconuts." That is men's work. The women of Kawaiahao cleaned the taro and cut it up, also grated the coconuts and squeezed the meat for its milk. Men took the taro chunks to the Kalihi Poi Mill for grinding.

Three days before the luau, three men including the *kahu's* son-in-law dug a six-by-six-foot *imu* (underground oven) in a far corner of the Kawaiahao Cemetery. Meanwhile, kahu showed his flock how to line five-gallon *mochi* tins with ti leaves, the stalks sticking up around the sides. Then he stirred the kulolo.

This is something like paddling the Molokai Canoe Race only it takes more muscle. He started with more than one hundred pounds of ground taro in a wash tub and kept stirring while helpers poured in 25 pounds of brown sugar, 15 pounds of honey, two bottles of Karo syrup and two gallons of coconut milk. Soon sweat beaded his brow. Every ten minutes, his daughter Sandy wiped him down with a towel. Ladies of the congregation nodded in approval. "Notice the men are doing all the work," said one woman complacently.

That was only the first batch. Son-in-law Bruce stirred the second batch while Kaina dipped the first batch into the mochi tins. Women tied the ti leaf stalks together one over the other. The tins went into the imu at 2 P.M. and came out at 11 A.M. By then, the workers could pull the kulolo out of the mochi tins just by lifting up on the crossed ti leaf stalks. Pretty smart, huh?

Kahu Kaina, after stirring the kulolo, was not too lively for a few days and he didn't make very many gestures during his sermon the following Sunday. "Last year I was so sore I had to take aspirin to sleep," he confessed.

Restoration of Kaena Point

Not all changes transport us into the future. Sometimes changes take us back to our past. This is especially true now that historic restoration of old buildings has become profitable. So I would like to tell the story of a recent historic restoration that is the first of its kind on Oahu and that was accomplished at absolutely no cost to anybody. Imagine if you can a project completed in the summer of 1988 that transported the entire island of Oahu back to the days of old Hawaii without spending a dime. Frankly, I didn't think it was possible. This is, after all, the space age. Everybody says you can't turn back the clock. Freeways girdle the island. Yet, for the first time in about 90 years, it is not possible to drive around the island. You have to walk.

This is because of the restoration, about 300 yards on the Makaha side of Kaena Point of the cliff. The old road, built by Benjamin F. Dillingham in 1899 as a railroad bed, finally washed out. What happened was not the slippage of a little soil. The whole road, for a stretch of about 30 feet, plunged into the sea, restoring the cliff to the way it was in the time of Kamehameha the Great.

It wasn't as if the washout interrupted traffic or anything. Everybody takes the short cut over the island from Haleiwa to Wahiawa. The old Kaena Point Road was at best a tenuous thread that bound the island together, an agony of ruts and boulders and dust and mud negotiable only with a four-wheel-drive vehicle. Yet it was THERE! And now it isn't. Now you have to walk to get around the island. It's a giant step backward.

I must admit that the old Kaena Point Road was considered a marvel of engineering when completed so long ago. Newspaper men invited by Dillingham to make the first run around the point on his railroad wrote poetic descriptions of the wilderness scenery. It was like a journey through the mountains for the roadbed had been blasted along cliffs that dropped steeply into a surging sea. When the railroad went bankrupt because of competition from trucks after World War II, the rails were torn up and the Kaena Road became a narrow, boulder studded track just wide enough for a Jeep.

So it remained for more than 40 years until the washout. As soon as I heard about it, I realized that a basic change had come to our island. I drove to the end of the paved road and on over dirt until the ruts got too bad. Then I parked behind a sand dune and walked. Soon I was trudging along under the gray-green cliffs, alone with the sea and the endless sky.

The road got worse and worse. I came to the point where the ocean currents meet, roiling the waves offshore, the point that divides the windward from the leeward shore. The strong, steady trade wind tugged at my clothes and kicked up whitecaps to the wind line. There, like magic, the ocean became placid and calm. I hiked around the point and out of the wind into sunbaked warmth. Then I came to the washout. It was peaceful there on the edge of the abyss, alone in that marvelous meeting of broad ocean and soaring cliff. Then I heard motorcycles. Mike and Bob Sinclair, two brothers from Kahaluu, came buzzing around Kaena Point from Mokuleia, the way I had come, on their dirt bikes. They screeched to a halt at the restoration project. The Sinclair brothers ride their

bikes wherever it is legal to ride. Potholes and ruts hold no terrors for them. Mud and loose dirt simply make the ride more interesting. But they peered over the edge at the wave-washed boulders below and shook their heads.

"Wow, look at that," said Mike. "We were out here two months ago. Four-wheelers couldn't make it anymore but you could still get around the washout on a two-wheeler." No more. Mountain goats can get by but I wouldn't want to do it on a horse. We stood there for a while and talked about it. The Sinclair brothers decided they didn't mind having the road closed since it was an act of God.

The State Department of Land & Natural Resources immediately took advantage of the washout to establish a Natural Area Reserve on Kaena Point. Michael Buck, a forester, said vegetation along the dunes had been so worn down by four-wheel-drive vehicles that the wind had blown away ten feet of sand in some places. So rock walls were placed across the road. Vehicles can drive no closer than half a mile from the point.

Buck said hiking and picnicking are encouraged and also the growth of vegetation and wildlife that has almost become extinct. A plant called *ohai* grows at Kaena Point and nowhere else on earth. It is the home for rare communities of *naupaka* and *ilima* and could become a home for the albatross, monk seals and green sea turtles.

Probably the most important effect of the washout is that it gets people out of their cars. Walking around Kaena Point instead of driving provides an entirely new perspective. You will notice before you have walked very far that your heart is beating faster and that you are breathing more deeply. It's because of something Kamehameha knew a lot more about than we do, exercise. You will notice also that the air is fresh and salty and that the view is magnificent. The cliffs soar above in silent, hoary splendor. Below, the ocean surges and heaves in perpetual fretfulness against the black lava shore.

The washout adds a whole new dimension to living on the island. It makes the land bigger knowing you can't whiz around in a a few hours. It creates a sense of mystery and invites the imagination to expand in a way that disappears on the freeway. The restoration of Kaena Point is more than a washout, it's a symbol of open space.

A Waikiki Lifestyle

Scott Hamilton, a twenty-five-year *kamaaina* of Waikiki, is a good example of a space-age beachcomber who has learned to survive in the most densely populated tropical paradise in the world. He moved to Waikiki when the skyline was still dominated by palm fronds. The landmarks he used to give directions by - Kau Kau Corner, Palm Tree Inn, Barefoot Bar – have long ago disappeared.

Why he lives in Waikiki and how he does it may be a valuable lesson for the future. Because Hamilton has proved that the age of individuality and exotic adventure in the midst of traffic and high rises is not dead. You just have to know where to look.

Hamilton is a retired urban planner, a bachelor in his sixties, and an Olympic class marathon runner which may be the reason he's still single. He'd rather run that eat, or anything else. For example, with the most famous beach in all the world in his back yard, he hardly ever goes near the water. Another reason he lives in Waikiki may be because he's an URBAN planner. Cities are his bailiwick. He's studied them all over the world. For that reason, his rules of thumb for how to cope with Waikiki's daytime population of 82,305 persons per square mile as a resident, not a visitor, should apply to city people everywhere. Here's his advice:

1. Don't drive a car.
2. Stay away from the condo as much as possible, take advantage of ALL the city.
3. Find anchors of continuity and havens of peace and use them.

"I find that I can't really relax in my Waikiki apartment," Hamilton explained. "My means of adapting is that I'm there only between 11 P.M. and 6 A.M., sleeping hours. That's fairly quiet." So at 6 A.M. Hamilton leaves his apartment overlooking the Ala Wai, a canal that defines Waikiki on the mountain side, and sets out running toward Diamond Head in the dark.

"The Ala Wai is one of the great canals of the world and it hasn't changed. It's an anchor of continuity," he explained. "It competes with the Grand Canal of Venice and the canals of London and Amsterdam. This canal is unique. You can stand at the Waikiki-Kapahulu Library (at one end of the canal) and look one and one-half miles over water. That's one reason local residents are violently opposed to a foot or auto bridge over the canal."

Hamilton said he runs up the brow of the hill behind Diamond Head just as the sun rises over Koko Head Crater far beyond. "It's a marvelous view," he said. "The sky is baby blue and the clouds are peach colored. Often I can see Molokai. Then I run to a convenience store in Waialae-Kahala (a posh suburb of Honolulu) and stick my head in the beer cooler to lower my body temperature before I have breakfast at the Yum Yum Tree at the Kahala Shopping Center."

As you have probably noticed by this time, Hamilton is not your run-of-the-mill resident of Waikiki. He quit his planning job with the Navy to prepare for the next 40 years because he figures he'll live to be at least a hundred. During the summer, he takes courses at Oxford and Cambridge.

"One reason I live in Waikiki is because the hotels are convenient for my friends who visit me from around the world," he said. "I have visitors several times a month. I tried living on Tantalus (a ridge on the mountains behind Honolulu) but it's too far from the hotels. Another reason I like Waikiki is because Kapiolani Park is the traditional center for long-distance running in Hawaii. It's so convenient, just roll out of bed for an event. Waikiki is also a bus terminus for all directions. I gave up having a private car in 1970. When I worked at Pearl Harbor, I ran home until carbon monoxide drove me off the road."

Hamilton spends most of his day at meetings downtown. Since he has a lot of correspondence, he goes to a little communications center where he can rent a typewriter or a word processor by the hour. It saves him the bother of having an office. There are lots of pleasant little places where he can eat. To relax, he goes to the Honolulu Club, a health spa.

His evening run takes him out of downtown along the waterfront to Magic Island, a public park on the ocean with tremendous views of the sea, the mountains, Waikiki and downtown Honolulu. It's another anchor. Then he runs back to the Honolulu Club for a shower.

He ends his day at the rotunda of the Hyatt Regency Waikiki when the band stops playing at Harry's Bar at 10 P.M. "The tourists leave and it's very peaceful, yet in the heart of Waikiki," he said. "In fact, I like it better than the Palm Court at the Plaza Hotel in New York where the vegetation is phony. The plantings at the Hyatt are real tropical jungle.

"I order a cafe au lait. They have a rack of newspapers like a Viennese cafe – the *Los Angeles Times*, *The Honolulu Advertiser*, *U.S.A. Today*, the *Wall Street Journal* and the *London Times*. So I read and drink by the waterfall. It's quiet and the sound of the water washes away the tension. I sort my mail and do my thinking before I go to bed."

114